LEADERSHIP EDUCATION AND TRAINING (LET 4)

With material selected from:

Developing Leadership Abilities,
by Arthur H. Bell and Dayle M. Smith

CUSTOM EDITION FOR ARMY JROTC
A Character and Leadership Development Program

PEARSON

Custom
Publishing

PEARSON CUSTOM PUBLISHING
75 Arlington Street, Suite 300, Boston, MA 02116
A Pearson Education Company

Brief Contents

Table of Contents

vi

Citizenship in Action

Unit 1

Chapter 2

Service to the Nation

Lesson 1

The Department of Defense

Key Terms

operational commands
specified
strategic
tactical
theater

What You Will Learn to Do

- Explore the purpose of the United States Department of Defense

Linked Core Abilities

- Do your share as a good citizen in your school, community, country, and the world

Skills and Knowledge You Will Gain along the Way

- Examine the mission of the Department of Defense (DoD)
- Identify the four major responsibilities inherent to DoD's mission
- Explain civilian control over the military
- Show the relationship between the Joint Chiefs of Staff and the DoD
- Define key words contained in this lesson

Introduction

The executive department responsible for the nation's defense forces is the Department of Defense (DoD). It was created in 1947 when Congress combined the former Navy and War departments into a National Military Establishment, an executive department headed by a secretary of defense. This lesson offers you an in-depth look at the DoD, what it does, and who works for it.

DoD's Roots

In 1789, Congress created the Department of War to administer and conduct military affairs. Congress separated the naval forces from the land forces in 1798, creating the Department of the Navy. The Departments of War and Navy remained for almost 150 years as the only two military departments; however, the *National Security Act* of 1947 created the Department of the Air Force and replaced the Department of War with the Department of the Army. This act also created the National Military Establishment to oversee the three Military Departments (Army, Navy, and Air Force — the Marine Corps was included under the Navy). In 1949, Congress renamed the National Military Establishment the Department of Defense. The seal for the Department of Defense is shown in Figure 2.1.1.

Missions

The mission of the Department of Defense is to "provide the military forces needed to deter war and protect the security of the United States." Inherent in this mission is the responsibility for planning military strategy, maintaining the armed forces, operating the military bases throughout the world, and defending the country from foreign threats. The Department of Defense assigns these duties to the Military Departments.

Figure 2.1.1: The official seal of the DoD.

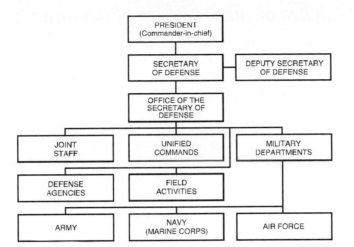

How the DoD Is Organized

The Department of Defense is the organization through which the President exercises civilian control over the military. The major elements of DoD are covered in the following sections and are shown in Figure 2.1.2.

Secretary of Defense

The Secretary of Defense, a civilian appointed by the President but subject to Senate approval, is the principal defense policy adviser to the President. Although the President has final authority and responsibility on all defense matters, the Secretary of Defense is responsible for formulating general defense policy, executing approved policy, and exercising authority, direction, and control over the DoD. The Annual Report to the President and Congress is the premier document issued by the Secretary of Defense. In addition to fulfilling a statutory requirement, it serves as an important reference document for many people interested in national defense issues and programs.

Note

The Secretary of Defense is sixth in the order of presidential succession, following the Vice President (VP), Speaker of the House, President Pro Tempore of the Senate (presiding officer of the Senate in the absence of the VP), Secretary of State, and Secretary of the Treasury. Beginning with the Secretary of State, succession is determined by the order in which the departments of the President's Cabinet were created.

Deputy Secretary of Defense

The Deputy Secretary of Defense is delegated full authority to act for the Secretary of Defense and to exercise the powers of the Secretary on any and all matters for which the Secretary is authorized to act pursuant to law.

Office of the Secretary of Defense

This office is the principal staff element of the Secretary of Defense in the exercise of policy development, planning, resource management, fiscal, and program evaluation responsibilities. The Office of the Secretary of Defense includes Under Secretaries for:

- **Acquisition and Technology — responsible for programs such as nuclear, chemical, and biological defense; acquisition reform; advanced technology; environmental security; logistics; space; and ballistic missile defense organization**
- **Comptroller — responsible for programs in areas such as contract audit, program analysis and evaluation, and national performance review activities**
- **Personnel and Readiness — responsible for programs such as force management, program integration, and health and reserve affairs**
- **Policy — responsible for programs such as international security affairs, special operations and low-intensity conflict, and strategy and threat reduction**

The Office of the Secretary of Defense also includes Assistant Secretaries for:

- **Command, Control, Communications, and Intelligence**
- **Legislative and Public Affairs**

Other elements of the Office include:

- **General Counsel**
- **Inspector General**
- **Director of Operational Test and Evaluation**

The central headquarters for the Department of Defense is at the world's largest office building, the Pentagon, located in Washington, D. C.

Joint Chiefs of Staff

The Joint Chiefs of Staff (JCS) constitute the immediate military staff of the Secretary of Defense and consist of the following general officers (four-star rank) from the Armed Forces:

- **Chairman (appointed by the President but subject to Senate approval)**
- **Vice Chairman**
- **Chief of Staff of the Army**
- **Chief of Naval Operations**
- **Chief of Staff of the Air Force**
- **Commandant of the Marine Corps**

The collective body of the JCS is headed by the Chairman, who sets the agenda and presides over JCS meetings. Additionally, the Chairman is the principal adviser to the President, Secretary of Defense, and the National Security Council.

All JCS members are, by law, military advisers, and they may respond to a request or voluntarily submit, through the Chairman, advice or opinions to the President, Secretary of Defense, or the National Security Council. Although responsibilities as members of the JCS take precedence over the duties as the Chiefs of the Military Services, these personnel are the senior military officers of their respective Services. As such, they are also responsible for keeping the Secretaries of the Military Departments fully informed on matters considered or acted upon by the JCS.

The main responsibilities of the Joint Chiefs of Staff, in conjunction with the Military Departments, include:

- **The strategic and tactical direction of the combatant forces**
- **The operation of the combatant forces under unified commands**
- **The integration of combatant forces into an efficient team of land, naval, and air forces**
- **Research and development**

Executive Authority

During World War II, the Joint Chiefs of Staff acted as executive agents in dealing with **theater** and area commanders, but the original *National Security Act* of 1947 saw the Joint Chiefs as planners and advisers, not as commanders of combatant commands. In spite of this, the 1948 *Key West Agreement* allowed members of the Joint Chiefs to serve as executive agents for unified commands, a responsibility that allowed them to originate direct communication with the combatant command.

Congress abolished this authority in a 1953 amendment to the *National Security Act*. Today, the Joint Chiefs have no executive authority to command combatant forces. The issue of executive authority was clearly resolved by the *Goldwater-Nichols DoD Reorganization Act* of 1986, which stated: "The Secretaries of the Military Departments shall assign all forces under their jurisdiction to unified and **specified** combatant commands to perform missions assigned to those commands ...;" the chain of command "runs from the President to the Secretary of Defense; and from the Secretary of Defense to the commander of the combatant command." The world is divided into nine geographical areas, each with a Commander-in-Chief (CINC) assigned. To facilitate mission accomplishment, these commanders have full **operational command** and control over all forces assigned to them.

Military Departments

The Military Departments of the Army, Navy, and Air Force are each headed by a Secretary who does not have cabinet rank and is a civilian. These Departments are responsible for maintaining the readiness of their assigned forces to ensure the security of the United States and to support the nation's policies and interests. The basic objectives of the Military Departments and the U.S. Armed Forces are to:

Key Note Term

strategic – of or relating to the large scale or global planning and conduct of military strategy, movements, and/or operations essential to the effective conduct of war.

tactical – of or pertaining to tactics

Key Note Term

theater – a large geographic area (including its land, sea, and air) in which active military operations are coordinated and conducted.

Key Note Term

specified – to state explicitly or in detail.

operational command – commands performing the primary mission of the service as distinguished from support commands.

- Prevent military actions that threaten the safety of the United States or its allies
- Defend the United States' territories, waters, and airspace
- Engage in all necessary military operations and other assigned duties
- End hostilities on terms favorable to the United States

Note

The Department of Defense maintains the academies for each of these Departments. Can you name these academies?

Conclusion

This lesson introduced you to the organization, background, and missions of the Department of Defense (DoD). You saw a specific example of the constitutional requirement for civilian control of the military with the President, Secretary of Defense, and the Secretaries of the Military Departments all being civilians. The highest military officers in the DoD are the Joint Chiefs of Staff. The missions and responsibilities of this Department make it a vital part of the federal government and critical to the nation's defense.

Chapter 2

Lesson Review

1. What is the mission of the DoD?
2. The Secretary of Defense is where in the line of presidential succession?
3. Identify one Under Secretary and the responsibilities for this position.
4. Define the term "theatre."

Lesson Review

Lesson 2

The Active Army

Key Terms

counterintelligence
doctrine
non-accession
unconventional

What You Will Learn to Do

- Relate the role of the Active Army to the United States Army

Linked Core Abilities

- Do your share as a good citizen in your school, community, country, and the world

Skills and Knowledge You Will Gain along the Way

- Explain how the two Congressional acts impact the organizational structure of Armed Forces
- Identify the Congressional act that provides basis for recent Army organization
- Distinguish between the fundamental roles of the Army and Active Army
- Identify how the Active Army contributes to domestic affairs
- Correlate Army commands to the JROTC program
- Determine categories under which the Army classifies its branches

- Classify the basic/special branches of the Army
- Identify two non-accession branches of the Army
- Define key words contained in this lesson

Introduction

The United States Army dates back to June 1775. On June 14, 1775, the Continental Congress adopted the Continental Army when it appointed a committee to "draft the rules and regulations for the government of the Army." This authorization marks the birthday of the U.S. Army, the oldest branch of the U.S. Armed Forces.

The Army is a major part of the U.S. Armed Forces, which collectively are responsible for defending American interests by:

- Supporting and defending the *Constitution* of the United States against all enemies, foreign and domestic
- Ensuring, by timely and effective military action, the security of the United States, its possessions, and areas vital to its interests
- Upholding and advancing the national policies and interests of the United States
- Safeguarding the internal security of the United States

Within that framework, the fundamental mission of the U.S. Army is to deter war and to win in combat; however, there is much more to the Army than accomplishing that mission. In fact, the Army spends most of its time involved in peacetime activities.

Origins of the U.S. Army

The legal basis for the establishment of the Army, as well as for the other branches of the armed forces, is set forth in the *Constitution*. The *Constitution* stipulates that the U.S. Armed Forces must answer to and be responsible for the needs and desires of the American people as expressed by their elected representatives. To achieve that, the Framers established the principle of civilian control over the military — that is, the President serves as Commander-in-Chief of the U.S. Armed Forces and Congress alone has the power to raise and support armies and to declare war.

Although the *Constitution* established the need for a system to "provide for the common defense," it did not define the organization of that system; therefore, in the course of our nation's history, the national defense structure has taken many forms. After the ratification of the *Constitution*, the newly formed Congress and President George Washington established the Department of War in 1789 as an executive department. The Secretary of War became its director and his powers were entrusted to him by the president.

Congress established our present military structure with the passage of two post-World War II legislations: the *National Security Act of 1947* and its *Amendments of 1949*. The 1947 Act:

- **Redesignated the Department of War as the Department of the Army, headed by the Secretary of the Army**

- **Created a separate Department of the Air Force and the U.S. Air Force as a branch of the armed forces**

- **Loosely grouped the Departments of the Army, Navy, and Air Force under the title of the National Military Establishment**

- **Established the Joint Chiefs of Staff, composed of the military chiefs of the three services, as a council to advise the three department secretaries and the president on military matters**

In 1949, Congress amended the *National Security Act of 1947* by passing the *National Security Act Amendments of 1949*. These amendments:

- **Established the Department of Defense (DoD) under the executive branch of the government and placed the Departments of the Army, Navy (including the Marine Corps), and Air Force subordinate to it.**

- **Established a Secretary of Defense to assist the president in providing direction, authority, and control of the three services. This secretary is appointed by the president and is a member of the president's cabinet.**

- **Stipulated that the president would appoint civilian secretaries to head of the Departments of the Army, Navy, and Air Force, and that those secretaries would come under the authority of the Secretary of Defense. These secretaries are responsible for, and have the necessary authority to conduct, all the affairs of their departments.**

- **Established a Chairman of the Joint Chiefs of Staff, also appointed by the president, who would have direct access to the Secretary of Defense.**

Note

To learn more about the Department of Defense and the Secretary of Defense, review Chapter 2, Lesson 1.

Following the passage of the *National Security Act* and its *Amendments*, Congress passed the *Army Organization Act of 1950*. This Act provides the legal basis for the present internal organization of the Army and the Department of the Army. It organizes the Army into a composite of commands, components, and branches — organized, trained, and equipped primarily for prompt and sustained combat operations on land. This act also:

- Stipulated that the president would appoint civilian secretaries to head of the Departments of the Army, Navy, and Air Force, and that those secretaries would come under the authority of the Secretary of Defense. These secretaries are responsible for, and have the necessary authority to conduct, all the affairs of their departments.

- Established a Chairman of the Joint Chiefs of Staff, also appointed by the president, who would have direct access to the Secretary of Defense.

The Army Concept

Under the Army concept, the U.S. Army consists of the active Army, the reserve components, and the Department of the Army civilian work force. The reserve components consist of the Army National Guard and the U.S. Army Reserve. The purpose of these components is to provide trained units and qualified personnel to be available for active duty in time of war, national emergency, or at other times as dictated by national security requirements.

Note

The reserve components are detailed later in this chapter.

A bond of mutual agreement exists among the active Army, the reserve components, and the Department of the Army civilian work force to ensure the operational effectiveness of the total Army. This bond promotes:

- **A balanced force structure**
- **Programs and projects designed to ensure modern equipment for both the active and reserve components**

There is cooperation and affiliation (teamwork) between active and reserve units, thus enhancing the mobilization potential of the reserve components and ensuring their timely availability to satisfy wartime reinforcement objectives.

Major Roles of the Total Army

In addition to its main mission — to deter war and to win in combat — the Army's major roles in executing U.S. military policies are:

- **To maintain the ability to respond to any level of aggression**
- **To be well-trained and equipped to prevent conflict**
- **To be employed at a level of strength necessary to ensure a swift and decisive end of the conflict if land forces are committed in combat**

- **To bring about an end to the conflict in terms favorable to the United States**
- **To fulfill a peacetime role by being able to contribute personnel and resources to domestic programs that support the general welfare of the people**

The Active Army

The active (or regular) Army is a component of the U.S. Army maintained by the federal government in peace and in war. Congress authorizes its strength yearly under the provisions of Article 1 of the *Constitution*. At the same time, Congress appropriates money for its sustainment, modernization, and pay.

Missions of the Active Army

The Army must be able to respond to threats that occur anywhere in the world. In addition, the Army supports security assistance programs conducted by the Departments of the State and Defense to friendly countries seeking economic and military assistance to maintain their stability and security. The Army makes an important contribution to those programs by providing military advisers, equipment, and other support. The results are positive because the Army's efforts are instrumental in implementing U.S. national security policies, and the Army shares in the benefits of mutual friendship, cooperation, and understanding — all of which serve the nation's interests.

Although maintaining national security is the determining factor in the need for an Army, the active Army also contributes in peacetime to the nation's general welfare through domestic involvement. However, Congress limits this involvement by law, tradition, and the need for the Army to maintain a high level of readiness to fulfill its primary mission. Some of the ways the Army contributes to domestic affairs are by:

- **Providing assistance to communities during natural disasters**
- **Assisting civilian communities during civil disturbances by providing personnel and equipment in support of civilian police forces**
- **Assisting civilian communities with civic-action programs**
- **Improving flood control and navigation**
- **Adding to the nation's scientific and technological skills through extensive research and development programs**
- **Advising and assisting governmental agencies in fighting the war on drugs**

Organization of the Active Army

The Department of the Army organizes the active Army in a number of ways. There are ten major commands in the Continental United States (CONUS) and four major commands located in Europe, Asia, and other regions of the world (OCONUS). The most well-known commands in CONUS are Forces Command

(FORSCOM) at Fort McPherson, Georgia, and Training and Doctrine Command (TRADOC) at Fort Monroe, Virginia. Other CONUS commands include:

- **Army Material Command**
- **Military District of Washington**
- **Medical Command**
- **Army Intelligence and Security Command (INSCOM)**
- **Criminal Investigation Command**
- **Corps of Engineers**
- **Military Traffic Management Command**
- **Army Special Operations Command**

OCONUS commands include U.S. Army Europe, U.S. Army Pacific, Eighth Army, and U.S. Army South.

FORSCOM controls all the combat and support units at installations throughout the United States.

TRADOC is responsible for developing Army **doctrine** and training. TRADOC also exercises control over the training installations throughout the United States. U.S. Army ROTC Cadet Command, a major subordinate command of TRADOC, manages both the Senior and Junior ROTC programs.

Branches of the U.S. Army

The Army classifies its units and personnel by branches. Branch names identify the types of units that personnel can select to enter (on enlistment) and the personnel who are trained in the primary functions of that branch. There are 17 basic and 8 special branches. The Army classifies 15 of the basic branches into the categories of combat arms, combat support, and combat service support. The remaining two, Special Forces and Civil Affairs, are **non-accession** branches. The eight special branches are all combat service support units.

Special Forces accomplish missions of **unconventional** warfare, foreign internal defense, direct action, strategic reconnaissance, and counterterrorism. Civil Affairs is only in the Army Reserve and it accomplishes missions of command, control, and coordination of civil-military operations.

COMBAT ARMS

The combat arms branches are directly involved in the conduct of actual fighting. The combat arms branches are as follows:

- **Infantry: Closes with the enemy by means of fire and maneuver, on foot or in armored vehicles, in order to destroy or capture the enemy or repel their assault by fire, close combat, or counterattack. Infantry is the nucleus around which the Army groups the other branches in combat operations.**

Key Note Term

doctrine – a principle (or creed of principles) relating to a specific belief, subject, theory, or branch of knowledge; the fundamental policy or standard for a principle or set of principles on a specific subject, theory, or branch of knowledge; something that is taught.

Key Note Term

non-accession – the policy or practice of not accepting personnel directly from traditional officer or enlisted entrance sources.

Key Note Term

unconventional – not bound by or in accordance with international agreements dealing with a specific subject, such as the rules or laws of warfare; The use of nuclear, biological, or chemical weapons or energy.

- **Armor:** Conducts mobile land and cavalry warfare; the tank is the nucleus of its forces.

- **Field Artillery:** Provides indirect fire support for the Infantry and Armor. Field Artillery uses cannons, missiles, and rockets and is capable of providing both nuclear and non-nuclear firepower.

- **Air Defense Artillery:** Provides air and missile defense on the battlefield by destroying enemy aircraft and missiles with automatic weapons or missiles.

- **Aviation:** Provides prompt and sustained combat air operations. Aviation units participate in a variety of combat and support roles including attack, assault helicopter, aerial observation, transportation, lift, supply, and troop transport duties.

- **Corps of Engineers:** Combat Engineer units are part of the combined arms team in combat operations. Corps of Engineers units provide combat support including construction, demolition, amphibious operations, defensive barriers, camouflage/ topographic activities, and minefield employment.

Note

Depending on their mission, engineer units can be a combat arms, combat support, or a combat service support branch.

COMBAT SUPPORT

The combat support branches provide operational assistance to the combat arms, and they participate in combat operations as part of the combined arms team. The combat support branches are as follows.

- **Corps of Engineers:** See description under combat arms.
- **Chemical Corps:** Provides the Army with highly trained people in nuclear, biological, and chemical (NBC) warfare defense programs. These programs include employment, logistical support, defensive procedures, equipment, training, scientific development, and management of NBC materials.
- **Signal Corps:** Provides command and control communications for Army forces. Signal units install, operate, and maintain communication-electronic equipment.
- **Military Police Corps:** Performs missions such as enforcing laws and regulations, conducting criminal investigative operations, securing U.S. government property, discharging of correctional functions, controlling traffic and movements, and securing critical areas and lines of communication.
- **Military Intelligence:** Plans, conducts, and supervises collection, analysis, production, and dissemination of intelligence, such as combat intelligence, and **counterintelligence** information pertaining to the enemy, weather, or terrain.

Key Note Term

counterintelligence – actions taken by intelligence personnel or units to prevent an enemy from gathering information about friendly forces, to deceive the enemy, to prevent sabotage, or to gather political and military information.

Note

The Signal Corps, Chemical Corps, and Military Police Corps can either be a combat support or a combat service support branch.

COMBAT SERVICE SUPPORT

The combat service support branches perform combat service support activities or administrative functions for the Army. These branches may also provide specialized services to other departments of the federal government and to the people of the United States.

The combat service support branches are as follows:

- **Adjutant General Corps:** Formulates policy and manages the Army's administrative and personnel systems.
- **Corps of Engineers:** See description under combat arms.
- **Finance Corps:** Is responsible for the management of the Army's financial resources, which includes paying U.S. Army personnel.
- **Quartermaster Corps:** Plans and directs the acquisition, receipt, storage, preservation, and issue of equipment, repair parts, fortification/construction material, subsistence, petroleum products, water, and other general supplies.
- **Signal Corps:** See description under combat support.
- **Chemical Corps:** See description under combat support.
- **Military Police Corps:** See description under combat support.
- **Ordnance Corps:** Is responsible for the maintenance and management of armament, tracked, wheeled, and general purpose vehicles, conventional and special munitions, test equipment, management of air defense and land combat missile systems, and construction material.
- **Transportation Corps:** Is responsible for the movement of personnel and equipment for the Army and for the Navy, Air Force, and government agencies as assigned.
- **Judge Advocate General's Corps:** Provides professional legal service and assistance in the fields of both military and civil law and supervises the Army's system of military justice.
- **Army Medical Department (includes Medical Corps, Dental Corps, Veterinary Corps, Army Nurse Corps, Army Medical Specialist Corps, and Medical Service Corps):** Provides medical, dental, and veterinary care. The chief functions of the Medical Department are: care of the sick and wounded, physical examinations, prevention of disease, and the operation of hospitals and dispensaries.
- **Chaplains:** The duties of the Army chaplains are similar to those performed by their civilian counterparts. They are clergymen from recognized denominational groups who have volunteered to perform their ministry in the Army. The mission of the Chaplains branch is to promote religion and morality in the Army by providing religious services, education, and counseling.

Note

The eight special branches of the Army are all combat service support units: the Judge Advocate General's Corps, Medical Corps, Dental Corps, Veterinary Corps, Army Nurse Corps, Army Medical Specialist Corps, Medical Service Corps, and the Chaplains.

Conclusion

This lesson covered the inception of the modern United States Army, from the adoption of the Continental Army in 1775 to current day. The concept of the U. S. Army includes the active Army, the reserve components, and the Department of the Army civilian work force, all of which work together to provide a balanced force structure as well as programs and projects designed to ensure modern equipment for both the active and reserve components. This lesson showed you the major roles of the total Army as well as the organization of the active Army.

Lesson Review

1. **Which document sets forth the legal basis for the establishment of the Army?**
2. **List the three concepts of the U. S. Army.**
3. **Choose one combat arms branch and explain it.**
4. **List three missions of the active Army.**

Chapter 2

Lesson Review

Lesson 3

The Army Reserve Components

Key Terms

citizen-soldiers
combatant
militia
mobilize
Reserve Corps

What You Will Learn to Do

* Distinguish among the reserve components of the United States Army

Linked Core Abilities

* Do your share as a good citizen in your school, community, country, and the world

Skills and Knowledge You Will Gain along the Way

* Identify the two Congressional acts that had an impact on the organization and structure of the Army reserve components

* Compare the missions of the Army National Guard and the Army Reserve

* Contrast the major types of units the Army National Guard and the Army Reserve contribute to the Army force

* Identify the three categories of the Army Reserve

* Define key words contained in this lesson

Recall that the reserve components of the U.S. Army consist of the Army National Guard and the Army Reserve. The main purpose of these components is to provide trained units and qualified personnel to be available for active duty in time of war, national emergency, or at other times as dictated by national security requirements.

The Army National Guard

The Army National Guard (ARNG) is one component of the Army (which consists of the Active Army, the Army National Guard and the Army Reserves.) The Army National Guard is composed primarily of traditional Guardsmen—civilians who serve their country, state and community on a part-time basis (usually one weekend each month and two weeks during the summer.) Each state, territory, and the District of Columbia has its own National Guard, as provided for by the Constitution of the United States.

The Army National Guard was founded on October 7, 1683, in the Massachusetts Bay Colony. The Massachusetts Bay Colony organized two units (one infantry regiment and one engineer battalion) as part of their local **militia**. These units also became part of the Continental Army during the Revolutionary War (1775–1783).

In August 1824, the New York State Militia was the first state to apply the term "National Guard." New York took the title as a compliment to the famous French hero, Marquis de Lafayette, who had commanded the French National Guard in Paris in 1789 and who had made great contributions in America's war for independence. Gradually, other states adopted the popular term for their units, and by 1896, only three states retained the word "militia" in their official designation.

The *National Defense Act of 1916* had a more profound impact on the Army National Guard than any other legislation of the past century. That Act and its amendments:

- **Officially designated state organized militias as the National Guard.**
- **Changed the organizational structure of the various National Guard units to conform to the structure of the active Army.**
- **Provided increased assistance from the federal government to the National Guard. Although the National Guard would still be under the control of state authorities, this legislation meant that when Guard units reached established Army standards, they became eligible for federal support.**

Another law passed by Congress in 1933 organized all Guard units into the National Guard of the United States; therefore, Congress made it possible for the Commander-in-Chief to give the National Guard an Army mission (or order) without having to wait for state governors to "call" those forces to duty.

In the late 1940s, Department of the Army established the Air National Guard, which was first used in the Korean War (1951–1953).

Key Note Term

militia – a citizen army— as distinct from a regular army or a body of full-time, professional soldiers—that is usually controlled by the individual states and subject to call during an emergency by the government of a country.

Throughout our proud history, as the Nation's oldest military organization, the Army National Guard has protected America—in war and peace—from all enemies, foreign and domestic.

Contribution to the Army Force and Its Missions

The National Guard has a unique dual mission that consists of both Federal and State roles. For state missions, the governor, through the state Adjutant General, commands Guard forces. The governor can call the National Guard into action during local or statewide emergencies, such as storms, fires, earthquakes, or civil disturbances.

In addition, the President of the United States can activate the National Guard for participation in federal missions. Examples of federal activations include Guard units deployed to Bosnia and Kosovo for stabilization operations, and units deployed to the Middle East and other locations in the war on terrorism. When federalized, Guard units are commanded by the Combatant Commander of the theatre in which they are operating.

Aiding America's Communities, Our State Mission

As previously mentioned, the Army National Guard exists in all 50 states, three territories, and the District of Columbia. The state, territory, or district leadership are the Commanders in Chief for each Guard. Their Adjutants General are answerable to them for the training and readiness of the units. At the state level, the governors reserve the ability, under the Constitution of the United States, to call up members of the National Guard in time of domestic emergencies or need.

The Army National Guard's state mission is perhaps the most visible and well known. Nearly everyone has seen or heard of Guard units responding to battle fires or helping communities deal with floods, tornadoes, hurricanes, snowstorms or other emergency situations. In times of civil unrest, the citizens of a state can rest assured that the Guard will be ready to respond, if needed. During 2001, 34,855 Guardsmen were called to duty in response to the needs of their community or state.

The Army National Guard is represented in more than 2,800 communities in 50 states, the District of Columbia, Guam, Puerto Rico and the Virgin Islands.

Organization of the Army National Guard

As part of the Army, the Army National Guard has to comply with Department of Defense and Department of the Army orders and regulations. Therefore, the Guard needs some way to gain access to the Secretary of the Army and the military chain of command (such as Army Chief of Staff). The organization that accomplishes this is the National Guard Bureau.

The National Guard Bureau (NGB) was formed to assist the states, territories, and District of Columbia procure funding for the Guard, administer policies and act as a liaison between the Departments of the Army and Air Force and the states.

The NGB is a joint bureau of the Departments of the Army and Air Force, and functions in both a staff and an operating capacity for each component. The

NGB performs the federal functions of the Army National Guard (ARNG) and the Air National Guard (ANG). The senior leader at NGB is the Chief, National Guard Bureau, usually a Lieutenant General.

The Army National Guard and the Air National Guard are each led by their own director. The two directors are selected by the Secretary of the Army (for the Director of the Army National Guard) and the Secretary of the Air Force (for the Director of the Air National Guard.) Both directors report to the Chief of the NGB. Full-time staffs support the Chief of the NGB and the directors of the ARNG and the ANG.

When ARNG units are not mobilized under federal control, they report to the Adjutant General of their state or territory, or in the case of the District of Columbia, the Commanding General. Each Adjutant General is responsible to the Governor of his state (or in the case of the District of Columbia, the mayor.)

Most members of the National Guard are part-time soldiers (referred to as **citizen-soldiers**). Typically, National Guard members are required to attend one drill weekend each month and one annual training period (usually two weeks in the summer) each year Weekend drills usually consist of one Saturday and Sunday each month, but occasionally include reporting for duty on Friday night. Initially, all non-prior service personnel are required to attend initial entry training (IET), also known as Basic Training. After Basic Training, soldiers go to their Advanced Individual Training (AIT) which teaches them the special skills they will need for their job in the Guard.

Accomplishments of the Army National Guard

Since its founding in the 1600s, the National Guard has participated in every American conflict to the current Iraqi War. In this century alone, Army National Guard units have fought and distinguished themselves in both World Wars, the Korean War, Vietnam War, the Persian Gulf War, Afghanistan, and now Iraq. In fact, individual Guardsmen received 14 Medals of Honor during World War II.

The National Guard plays a vital role in the Army, it must be ready to **mobilize** and deploy on very short notice. The Sept. 11th terrorist attacks on the United States resulted in the activation of thousands of Army Guard personnel. A total of 9,600 National Guard men and women were already on duty across the country Sept. 14, 2001 when President George Bush approved an order to call up as many as 50,000 members of the National Guard and Reserves. Soon after the attacks Army Guard soldiers were ordered to the Nation's airports to assist in security. Governors of many states also called on the Guard to protect critical facilities and infrastructure. The mission of Homeland Security for the Guard is not a new mission, nor is it the only mission; it is only one of the many missions of the Guard.

President Bush's call for a temporary tour of active duty for up to 50,000 National Guard and Reserve troops in a military operation on American soil is the largest of its kind since 1916.

Army National Guard soldiers were an essential element in controlling wildfires throughout the western United States. Many of the Guard troops were called August 2001 to assist civilian firefighters in Oregon, Nevada, Montana, California, South Dakota, Arizona and Washington.

Key Note Term

citizen-soldiers – members of the National Guard or Army Reserve Corps.

Key Note Term

mobilize – to assemble, prepare, or put into operation (personnel, units, equipment, and so on) for war or a similar emergency.

In 1996 and 1997, National Guard personnel deployed overseas to support **combatant** commands and U.N. peacekeeping forces and soldiers from 16 states and territories participated in a record 160 state emergency call ups and local civil authority missions.

Today's National Guard is better trained and equipped to respond to any state or national emergency than at any time in its history. In peacetime, National Guard units train alongside active Army commands or units for which the Army has associated them through partnership agreements. In the event of mobilization, these Guard units would then deploy and serve with their active Army units during wartime. The Army simply cannot enter into a major conventional war without the support of the Army National Guard.

The U.S. Army Reserve (USAR)

Public attitude and economics played an important role in the origins of the Army Reserve. In our country's early days, citizens were suspicious of a large active Army, and they knew it would be difficult to financially support such a large standing army. Therefore, a reserve military structure became attractive because it provided a capability to mobilize military forces when the situation arose.

The USAR originated on April 23, 1908, the result of lessons learned from the Spanish-American War and the realization that the Regular Army could not provide enough medical personnel to take care of the needs of an expanded wartime force. Its beginnings were quite modest: commissions as first lieutenants were initially given to 160 Army contract physicians who became the first members of the federal reserve corps. From that small beginning has grown the modern day Army Reserve of thousands of units and hundreds of thousands of well-trained men and women.

The *National Defense Act of 1916* formally established the **Reserve Corps**. It also established the Junior Reserve Officers' Training Corps (JROTC), provided for an Officers' Reserve Corps through direct commissioning up to the grade of major, and formulated a Reserve Officers' Training Program at civilian colleges and universities.

The *Reserve Forces Act of 1955* reorganized the Army Reserve. It was important legislation because although federal budget cuts forced the active Army to cut its strength, that act increased the size of the Army Reserve (despite eliminating 15 Army Reserve divisions) and stipulated that Reserve units would receive more modern equipment over a 15-year period.

Contribution to the Total Army Force and Its Missions

The Army Reserve proved itself during World War I, when over 160,000 officer and enlisted Reservists served their country. World War II saw over 200,000 Reserve officers take part in the war. These officers, in the words of Army Chief of Staff General George C. Marshall, "constituted the principal available asset

---

Key Note Term

combatant – engaged in combat.

Key Note Term

Reserve Corps – trained military members available to augment active duty forces in times when activated.

which we possessed at this time. Without their assistance, the program (expansion of the Army) could not have been carried out except in a superficial manner." The Korean War, and to a much lesser extent, Vietnam, also saw Army Reserve involvement.

The USAR really proved itself, though, during Operation Desert Shield/Desert Storm, when tens of thousands of Army Reservists and hundreds of units were called up and sent to the Persian Gulf region. It is fair to say that the victory in the Gulf could not have occurred without the contributions of the Army Reserve.

The Army Reserve has two major missions:

1. **To organize, train, equip, and provide units to help defend our nation with little or no advance notice in the event that Congress or the president mobilizes the armed forces.**

2. **To provide trained individual reinforcements, officer and enlisted, as prescribed by Department of the Army mobilization plans. These soldiers would replace initial battlefield casualties, reinforce active Army units, and provide reinforcement for reserve component units that are mobilized.**

Organization of the Army Reserve

Unlike the National Guard, the Army Reserve is under federal control during peacetime. As a part of the total Army, it fulfills the Army's need for units to meet its mission requirements in times of changing national priorities and limited resources. Recently, an Army Chief of Staff remarked that the active Army could not be successfully committed to a major conflict in Europe without the Army Reserve.

The Chief of the Army Reserves is an adviser to the Army Chief of Staff on Army Reserve matters. Therefore, U.S. Army Reserve Command (USARC) channels begin at Department of the Army and flow through Forces Command (FORSCOM) to the 10 Regional Support Commands (RSCs), the three Regional Support Groups (RSGs), and to the three Army Reserve Commands (ARCOMs) located outside the Continental United States.

The USAR is organized into three unique categories: Ready Reserve, Standby Reserve, and the Retired Reserve.

Ready Reserve

The Ready Reserve consists of the Selected Reserve and the Individual Ready Reserve (IRR).

The Selected Reserve consists of members assigned to Troop Program Units (TPU), Individual Mobilization Augmentation (IMA) Program positions and the USAR portion of the Active Guard/Reserve (AGR) Program. The AGR Program offers Army Reserve soldiers an opportunity to serve in active duty positions supporting USAR programs. Here's how each works.

TPUs enjoy the adventure and camaraderie of soldiering while serving in a reserve status. TPUs are located throughout the United States and even overseas. Usually TPUs train just one weekend a month, plus two weeks' Annual Training. Normally, this comes out to only 38 days per year.

IMA affiliates with a particular active Army unit, assigned to a unit duty position, and wear the unit patch and insignia. They train with the unit at least two weeks during the year and are eligible for many USAR benefits, including the Montgomery GI Bill for the Selected Reserve.

The Ready Reserve includes troop program units and the Individual Ready Reserve that are liable for active duty as prescribed by law. The highest priority elements are the members of the troop program units who are in a paid drill status. More than 3,200 units of company or detachment size are located throughout the 50 states, Puerto Rico, Guam, and Europe. The Individual Ready Reserve consists of members not assigned to a unit, but they can be mobilized by order of the president in response to a national emergency.

Each troop program unit is required to conduct 48 training assemblies (or drills) annually. For every four-hour drill, the unit member receives one day's pay and one retirement point. Drills are usually conducted as four training assemblies one weekend per month at the unit's reserve center or at a training site. In addition, each unit performs at least 14 days of annual training.

The IRR is composed of trained individuals assigned to a central pool. These Reservists will augment and fill active Army and Army Reserve units should there be a call for mobilization.

The IRR is made up of two groups. The first group is the USAR Control Group (Annual Training). The Annual Training Group consists of non-unit members (with less than three years of active duty) who have a military service/training obligation to complete.

The second group is the USAR Control Group (Reinforcement). The Reinforcement Group is comprised of non-unit members (over three years of active duty) with no training requirements.

Standby Reserve

The Standby Reserve are those units and members of the reserve components (other than those in the Ready Reserve or the Retired Reserve) who are liable for active duty only in time of declared war or national emergency. The Standby Reserve is composed of Reservists who have completed all Ready Reserve obligations, but who have yet to complete their eight-year military service obligation. Members of the standby reserve can be in an active or an inactive status.

Active status refers to reservists who are completing their statutory military service obligation; were screened from the Ready Reserve as being key personnel; or may be temporarily assigned to the Standby Reserve for hardship reasons.

Inactive status refers to individuals who are not required by law or regulation to remain members of an active status program but who desire to retain their Reserve affiliation in a non-participating status, or have skills that may be of possible future use to the Army.

Retired Reserve

The Retired Reserve consists of individuals that completed a total of at least 20 years of creditable Federal Military Service in either the active Army, or one of the Reserve Components whom the Army placed on a Reserve Retired list. In all cases, the last eight years must have been spent in a Reserve Component.

The Army may involuntarily order any of those people, if qualified, to active duty in time of declared war or national emergency when the Secretary of the Army determines that adequate numbers of qualified individuals are not available in the Ready or Standby Reserves.

Accomplishments of the Army Reserve

Since its establishment in 1916, reservists have served in both World Wars, the Korean War, the Berlin Crisis, the Vietnam War, the Persian Gulf War, and now in Iraq. In fact, of the personnel mobilized for the Korean War over one-half were reservists. Additionally, during the U.S. Postal Service strike in 1970, the U.S. government called 8,000 reservists to active duty to help deliver the mail. They are currently answering the call in Bosnia and other places around the globe, carrying the torch passed on by the citizen-soldiers two hundred years before who left their homes, farms, and businesses to take up arms against tyranny.

Conclusion

From its formal origination in 1908 to now, Army Reservists have played a vital role in our nation's defense. From the hedgerows of World War I to the desert sands of the Persian Gulf, when our country needed its citizen-soldiers, they were there.

A distinguishing feature of the USAR is the important contribution Reservists make in the cities, towns and villages in which they live and work. Their excellent training and varied experience make them valuable members of their communities. Often, Reservists put in long hours at such diverse projects as, running medical clinics, clearing land for play grounds, and they stand ready to help in times of crisis or national emergency. Their contributions of time, energy and skill can make their towns a better place to live.

If you are considering a career in the active Army or one of the reserve components of the U.S. Army, you should now have a better understanding of their roles and structure. More important, you now should have an idea of the role that the Army plays in our American society.

Lesson Review

1. What state was the first to apply the term "National Guard"?

2. Compare and contrast the National Guard and the Army Reserves.

3. What are the three major categories of the Army Reserves?

4. Define the term "citizen-soldiers."

Leadership Theory and Application

Unit 2

Chapter 6

Leadership Principles

Lesson 1

Power Bases and Influence

Key Terms

coercive power
defensive
developmental
expert power
legitimate power
referent power
relinquishing
reward power

What You Will Learn to Do

- Outline a personal plan to build strong relationships with team members

Linked Core Abilities

- Take responsibility for your actions and choices
- Apply critical thinking techniques

Skills and Knowledge You Will Gain along the Way

- List the different types of power and influence
- Describe the appropriate application of power and influence
- Discuss how individual and system power can be used to increase performance
- Define key words contained in this lesson

Introduction

Leaders can often experience tremendous confusion as they exercise power and influence. If they provide too little influence, their followers will drift aimlessly. If they exert too much power, the follower will shut down. In this lesson you learn about the bases of power available to leaders and how to use them effectively. You will also learn about four different approaches to influencing.

Power is the capacity to which you can influence someone else to behave in accordance with what or how you want them to. The amount of power you have is contingent on the level of dependency that person has on you. The greater the dependency, the greater the power. You only have power if you have something that the other person wants. As a high school student living at home, you are highly dependent on your parents for financial support. Once you graduate and get a job, the level of dependence significantly decreases.

The two concepts of leadership and power are closely intertwined yet have important differences. Leadership focuses on the attainment of a goal. Power does not need to have a goal, just dependence. Leadership most often refers to a downward influence and power does not. Power is focused on gaining compliance.

Source of Power

A leader can experience confusion and frustration when trying to gauge how and when to exert power. Leaders used to draw their power from the fact that they were the "boss." The followers were dependent on the leader for distribution of rewards and punishments; however, it has been learned that leading from the position of boss with these controls can yield average performance. To energize followers, leaders must grasp a broader understanding of and relationship to power. Five power bases from which power is yielded include coercive, reward, legitimate, expert and referent.

Coercive power is defined as a power that is yielded by fear — fear that negative results might occur if one does not comply. Fear is generated from the belief that someone might inflict pain, restrict movement or withhold basic needs.

Reward power is seen when people comply with the wishes of another because they may be given something of value in return — that there is a positive benefit for doing so.

Legitimate power is given to the person in the position within the hierarchy. Positions of authority can use both coercive and reward power. Most often, because of the position they hold, when they speak, the followers listen and comply.

Expert power comes from the result of specific expertise, knowledge or special skills. Those who exert expert power are seen as the expert in the field (such as technology, medicine, politics, and religion) and their advice is sought after and followed.

Key Note Term

coercive power – power that is yielded by fear.

reward power – when people comply with the wishes of others to get something in return.

legitimate power – power given to the person in the position within the hierarchy.

expert power – power resulting from specific expertise, knowledge, or special skills.

Referent power is based on admiration. This power is used often in the advertising world. Tiger Woods is admired by the world and can influence what people buy through his endorsement of the product. The product is purchased in hopes to be seen more like him.

Table 6.1.1 shows examples of the different types of power covered in this lesson.

Key Note Term

referent power – a type of power that is used to influence others.

Table 6.1.1: Examples of Power

coercive	The person yells at others and you want to avoid making him angry.
reward	The person gives rewards to people and you want to trade favors with him.
legitimate	The person is the supervisor and you are the subordinate and she has the right to ask for compliance.
expert	The person has the knowledge and experience in the task at hand and you defer to her judgment.
referent	You really like this person and search for opportunities to do things for him.

Understanding Influence

Influence can be thought of as power in action. It is difficult to know how much influence to exert with followers and in teams. The challenge is to know when and how to exercise more or less influence on the follower or the team. Four types of influence available to the leader are: controlling, relinquishing, developing, and defensive.

Controlling is a one-way approach. It involves exerting pressure, using authority or attempting to persuade someone into doing something the way you feel it should be done.

It is best to use this approach when you have all or most of the facts, experience, or knowledge related to the problem at hand, there is an emergency situation or speed is important, the resistance to a course of action is low, and/or the need to develop collective commitment and understanding is low.

Even if you have all the facts, unless others recognize your expertise (expert power), they will resist the controlling approach. There are a few situations where any one person has all the facts or knowledge related to the problem. No one of us is as smart as all of us. And finally, this method is less effective when there are expectations of employee involvement.

Key Note Term

relinquishing –
giving up;
submitting.

Relinquishing is also a one-way approach and it involves giving up influence and reducing one's contribution or role in the situation. The leader may accommodate or comply with the wishes of others. This one-way approach puts others in the influencing position.

It is best to use this approach when the team has most of the facts and experience related to the problem, the problem is highly personal and not work-related, and/or the team is highly motivated and can learn from the experience.

Be careful that you are not using the relinquishing approach to avoid "rocking the boat." Sometimes discussions are hard and people are not always happy. Don't use this approach to avoid dealing with the issue. If you have been controlling and feel the need for change, don't run all the way to this point to compensate from previous behavior.

Key Note Term

developmental –
sharing opinion of
fact.

The **developmental** approach is a two-way or mutual approach. It involves sharing opinions or facts. This approach is used most often when there is a need for consensus.

This approach is best used when the individuals involved do not have all the experience and knowledge about the situation, collective commitment is important, there is resistance or a difference of opinion, and/or new ideas are needed.

Just a word of caution here. The developmental approach takes more time and energy on the part of everyone. Some may feel this is a rather soft approach and may be uncomfortable with it. It is important that you have strong communication and listening skills.

Key Note Term

defensive –
withdrawing.

The **defensive** approach occurs when the person withdraws from the situation. This withdrawal can be seen visibly by someone leaving the room, or invisibly, by tuning people out. The person in this behavior cannot be influenced or influence others.

This approach is best used when there is insufficient information to explore the issue any further, and/or there is a legal, moral, or ethical consideration that prevents discussion of the issue. But patience is important here. Don't continue to push and if withdrawal occurs, be willing to come back at another time to better understanding of the situation.

Different situations require you to select the appropriate approach; used appropriately, each approach can be effective. Effective two-way communications and a win/win attitude about conflict are key ingredients to the developmental approach and most often the benefits of the developmental approach out weigh the others. When in the developmental approach process there is a great amount of give-and-take of information, ideas, and opinions between the leader and the follower or the team. If disagreement exists, instead of saying you don't agree, explore the reasons behind the idea. You could ask "Why do you think that is important? What would happen if we did that?" The assumption that one person is right or wrong is set aside and all ideas are considered. There is a desire to hear what is being said. Clearly this is not the type of influence you are most likely familiar with. You might be more used to the controlling (being told what to do) or the relinquishing (withdrawing from the discussion). You might also be used to how those two approaches feel to you; after you experience the developmental approach, as either the leader or the follower, you will want to lead or follow that path again.

As a leader in an organization you will often feel caught between the needs of your organization and the needs of your team for they are not always the same. The beginning of this lesson defined power as "the capacity to influence people," and you learned about where power comes from and different approaches to influencing others. You can broaden this definition and its application. An expanded definition of power can be "the capacity to influence the larger system to survive and adapt." It is important that you know how to use the power and influence you have in your organizational role as well as the role of team/unit leader. You will have information from different parts of the organization and can see the total picture more clearly than either the team or the organization. It is your responsibility to facilitate integration of both viewpoints.

Leaders can serve an integrating function by moving back and forth between working with their teams and working with other team leaders in the organization. When you are with your team you are working independently from other team leaders. You will use your influencing skills within your team. You will focus on what is working, what the team needs, and what difficulties the team is experiencing. When you are meeting with other team leaders, however, there is a sharing of what they have heard while working with their own teams.

The potential knowledge pool for team leaders is substantial. Team leaders create a forum for sharing information with each other and affecting the organization as a whole. Often this is known gaining "critical mass."

Conclusion

In this lesson you learned about the bases of power available to leaders and how to use them effectively. You also learned about four different approaches to influencing people.

Lesson Review

1. **List and give brief explanations of the five power bases.**
2. **Compare and contrast relinquishing and developing influence.**
3. **What is the difference between leadership and power?**
4. **What is the main downside to controlling influence?**

Chapter 6

Lesson Review

Lesson 2

Styles of Leadership

Key Terms

directing
delegating
leadership style
participating

What You Will Learn to Do

- Assess personal leadership style

Linked Core Abilities

- Take responsibility for your actions and choices
- Apply critical thinking techniques

Skills and Knowledge You Will Gain along the Way

- Describe different styles of leadership
- Explain which leadership styles are best suited for different situations
- Identify ways to improve management skills
- Define key words contained in this lesson

Introduction

To command respect and obedience as a leader, you must be prepared to lead. Because your actions and attitudes set the example for others to follow, you must also be ready for any type of situation that may occur. Therefore, how you lead — or your style of leadership — can mean the difference between success or failure of a mission. This lesson introduces you to three basic leadership styles: **directing**, **participating**, and **delegating**. You will have the opportunity to develop a style that works for you as you progress in rank in Army JROTC.

Leadership styles are the pattern of behaviors that one uses to influence others. You can influence others in many different ways. Those patterns will be perceived by others as your **leadership style.**

It's important to understand the differences between autocratic and democratic styles of leadership as well as sources of leadership behavior. Autocratic leaders use positional power and direct authority to influence others; democratic leaders use personal power and involve their followers in the decision-making and problem–solving processes. You can use a continuum with autocratic on one end and democratic on the other to learn if your style is either one or the other. When the historical perspective of leadership was discussed in the lesson, "Leadership Reshuffled," you learned that leadership styles did not have to be an either/or set of behaviors. In fact you learned that the situation the leader was faced with affected his/her choice of behaviors.

Think of your classmates who are leaders: the student body president, the cadet battalion commander, and group project leaders. These individuals have certain responsibilities so they can accomplish their goals. The manner in which they carry out those responsibilities and the way they interact with others is their style of leadership. The three basic leadership styles are directing, participating, and delegating.

Key Note Term

directing – a leadership style where the leader tells team members what to do and how to do it.

participating – a leadership style where the leader consults with, obtains advice from, or asks the opinions of one or more followers before making a decision.

delegating – a leadership style where the leader delegates problem-solving and decision-making authority to a teammate or to a group of followers.

leadership style – patterns of behavior that a leader uses to influence a team or group of followers.

Directing Style

Leaders use the directing leadership style when they tell their team members what they want done and how, when, and where they want it done, without getting others' advice or ideas. They then supervise closely to ensure team members follow their directions precisely.

This style is clearly appropriate when:

- **Time to complete the mission is short and only you know what needs to be done and how to do it.**

- **You must lead people who lack experience at a certain task and you must direct their behavior.**

Normally, most people will not resent this close supervision because you will be giving them exactly what they need and want.

> ### Note
>
> Sometimes people think that leaders are using the directing style when they yell, scream, threaten, or intimidate followers. This is not a directing style — it is simply an abusive, unprofessional way to treat people. Do not confuse emotion or anger with styles of leadership.

> ### Case 1
>
> Jon is normally an average student; however, when he takes charge of a group to complete a project, his work and the finished effort of the group are always outstanding.
>
> When asked about his group's results, his teammates proudly answer, "Jon makes it easy for us to complete our tasks. He helps us and makes suggestions when we need help, but he lets us do the work. If we have a problem, he always listens to our ideas on how to fix it.
>
> "Because he is always excited about what he is doing, we get excited, too. He seems to know all he can about a task before we get started on it. While we are doing the task, he respects our views about how to complete it, he effectively uses the talents of everyone on the team, and he makes smart decisions. He is always there for us if we need him and, somehow, he still finds the time to do his share of the project. Because of his effective work habits, he instills good work habits in us also.
>
> "He accepts responsibility for the outcome of our tasks, whether good or bad. None of us want a project to be done poorly, but he does not blame others for any mistakes that he or the team may have made. After finishing one task, we are always glad to begin the next project under his direction."

Participating Style

Leaders use the participating style when they consult with, obtain advice from, or ask the opinions of one or more followers before making a decision. Although leaders may ask for such information or recommendations, they are still the ones who make, and are responsible for, the final decision.

This style is appropriate for leadership situations when those whom you are leading are fairly competent and support your goals. Allowing them to participate can be a powerful team-building process. It will increase confidence and support if everyone has a part in developing the final plan.

Do not think that obtaining good advice from a teammate or using another member's plan or idea is a sign of weakness on your part. It is a sign of strength that your followers will respect; however, you are responsible for the quality of your plans and decisions. If you believe that your follower's idea is not a good one, you must reject it and do what you believe is right, regardless of pressure to do otherwise.

Case 2

Marla knows exactly what her position is all about. She gets excited whenever an instructor assigns her a project because she knows that she can get it done. Sometimes, she even suggests projects to her instructor. Based on her ideas, the instructor usually assigns them to her and her team.

Marla is highly motivated and has very structured work habits. She likes to map out a project in which everything is her decision. She then tells her team members how to do each step of their tasks according to her direction. She watches everything that her team members do, and if they appear to be doing a task differently from her plan, she criticizes them.

Marla got upset once when a teammate was caught stealing. At first, she was afraid to talk to that person about the incident, and she did not know what to say to her peers who had also heard about it. Finally, after asking herself how she would like to be treated if she were the one involved, she called a team meeting.

At the meeting, Marla informed everyone that all team members make mistakes, not only as a team but also as individuals. She hoped that if they ever had any problems, they would turn to her and/or to another team member for help. They agreed.

Delegating Style

The delegating style is the most efficient. It requires the least amount of your time and energy to interact, direct, and communicate with your team members. Leaders use the delegating style when they delegate problem-solving and decision-making authority to a teammate or to a group of followers.

This style is appropriate when:

- **Dealing with mature followers who support your goals and are competent and motivated to perform the task delegated.**
- **Certain key members of your team are able to analyze a problem or situation, determine what needs to be done, and do it.**

Remember, you are still responsible for the results of their actions and decisions.

Case 3

Brian is an easy-going person. He wants to complete projects with plenty of time left so that he and his friends on the team can relax. After he assigns tasks to each of his team members, he lets them figure out the best way to complete the tasks — without giving them any help, direction, or supervision. Plus, he rarely makes any decisions.

Then, when the time comes to complete the project, he still turns it in even though parts of it are not finished. When the final grade comes back, his group makes the lowest mark in the class, prompting an instructor to ask, "Why wasn't your project done?"

Brian passes the blame on to his team members by saying, "They didn't complete their parts as they should have. I don't believe that I should have to be responsible for or receive a bad grade because of their sloppy efforts."

When the other team members find out their grades, they approach Brian, "Why didn't you tell us everything that we were supposed to do? We could have worked harder and done it better if we had just known."

Keep in mind that no one style is superior to another. What works in one situation may not work in another. You must develop the flexibility to use all three styles and the judgment to choose the style that best meets the situation and the needs of your team. In fact, you may want to use all three styles or different styles:

- **With different followers or in different situations.**
- **When you receive a new project, you receive new personnel, or your supervisor changes.**
- **If the competence, motivation, or commitment of your team changes.**

Do not fall into the trap of believing that there are some leadership techniques that must always work. You must evaluate every situation carefully when choosing the right style. Keep in mind that the best strategy in one situation may be inappropriate in another.

Situational Leadership Model

Ken Blanchard and his colleagues built upon existing research and continued discussions with successful leaders on how the follower affected leadership behaviors. They developed the Situational Leadership Model from their research. This model identifies four leadership styles (sets of behaviors) and four developmental levels of the followers and the relationship between the two.

Note

To learn more about Ken Blanchard, his background, his books, and his company, check out www.kenblanchard.com.

The leadership styles in this model are based on the leader providing either directive or supportive behaviors.

Directive behavior is defined as how much structure, control, and supervision the leader provides to the follower.

Supportive behavior is defined as how much praise, listening, and facilitating the leader provides the follower.

These styles also vary in three ways: the amount of direction given, the amount of encouragement and support provided, and the amount of involvement the follower has in decision-making.

The four styles are known as:

Style 1	Directing
Style 2	Coaching
Style 3	Supporting
Style 4	Delegating

They are similar to the three styles discussed earlier in this lesson.

The behaviors that are present when using Style 1 will be more directive and less supportive. The follower will be told what, how, when, and where to do the task. There is little to no involvement from the follower in decision-making. Communication is one-way.

The behaviors present when using Style 2 will be providing equal amounts of directive and supportive behaviors. Here, the leader will provide lots of direction, but will ask the follower for ideas and suggestions. A more two-way communication style exists; however, the leader is still in control of the decisions.

Style 3 behaviors are high supportive and low directive. While using this style the leader allows the follower to take control of the day to day decisions. The leader's job is to listen and facilitate the problem-solving process. The decision-making process begins to shift from the leader to the follower.

Style 4 requires low supportive and directive behaviors. Here the leader behaviors change to allowing the follower to make the decisions on how to solve an agreed upon situation or task.

You learned earlier in this lesson that there is no ONE best way to lead. The most effective leader matches his/her behaviors to the situation and the follower. The amount of decision making and involvement the leader allows the follower depends on the situation or the task (have they ever been in this situation before or done this task before) and the level of confidence and competence (how sure of and how skilled in performing the task) the follower possesses.

Now that you know the four leadership styles and the pattern of behaviors in each, turn to the four developmental levels of the followers. These levels are based on the competence (the level of knowledge to do the task) and commitment (a combination of confidence and motivation).

The development level of the follower is based on his/her level of competence and confidence. There are four developmental levels:

Level 1	low
Level 2	low to moderate
Level 3	moderate to high
Level 4	high

Level 1 exists when the follower has a high level of commitment (very motivated and confident) with a low level of competence (knowledge of how the task is to be done). An example of this situation can be your first day of drill in the leadership lab. You were probably most excited and motivated to perform as a platoon leader or sergeant. You did not know how to perform this task, but you were committed to making it happen. It required your leader to give you exact directions on how to do the task. You listened and did what you were told so you could learn the routines. The leader matched his style of leadership to your developmental level.

Level 2 happens after you have been given direction and you have practiced enough to feel competent to perform the task. Your level of commitment to practice begins to drop. You are getting somewhat bored with the repetition of drill. This level is described with having low commitment and some competence. The leadership style now needs to change from directing to coaching. Letting you get involved in the process and asking for ideas, suggestions, or shared leadership will be more effective at this time. The focus here is to keep your confidence on the rise while recharging your commitment. You are not ready to take charge yet and the leader recognizes you still need direction and practice to be able to perform outstandingly.

Level 3 is when you have high competence (the ability to perform well) but your commitment level is not consistent. The supporting leadership style is more appropriate now. It is time to get you involved in making the task happen and shifting the responsibility from the leader to the follower. Again, the follower can perform the task, but for some reason is not highly committed to making it happen. The focus is to keep the performance high AND consistent.

Level 4 is when the follower is highly committed and highly competent in performing the task. The follower not only knows how to perform the task well, but WANTS to perform the task well. The leader will focus on recognizing the performance.

As you progress through the JROTC program, you will be asked to take a leadership role in the leadership lab where you can practice the directing, coaching, supporting and delegating role with new cadets. You will also be involved in service community projects that will allow you to practice the leadership styles. These assignments will be made based on YOUR performance and developmental level. You will be very competent at drilling tasks; however, this may be the first time you will experience a leadership role. You will be energetic and motivated because you know how to drill; however, the task of leading others in drill is new to you and you will need direction from your instructor so you can build your competence and commitment through the process. As you become better skilled in matching leadership style to developmental level, your instructor will begin to coach, support, and finally, delegate the role of leadership to you.

When in a leadership position, you must assess your team's capability to perform its mission, and then develop a plan that accomplishes it. You should use the style that your experience tells you is most appropriate after you have assessed the team's level of competence, motivation, and commitment to accomplish its mission.

A good rule of thumb to follow is to be flexible in your thinking. Approach each leadership situation as an opportunity to improve your leadership potential, ability, and style.

Conclusion

As you have learned, leadership styles are the pattern of behaviors that one uses to influence others. You now know that you can influence others in many different ways. Those patterns are perceived by others as your leadership style.

Chapter 6

Lesson Review

1. **Compare and contrast the directing, participating, and delegating styles of leadership.**
2. **Which directing style do you feel best suits you as a leader? Why?**
3. **List the four styles of the situational leadership model.**
4. **Choose two developmental levels of followers and explain them.**

Lesson Review

Lesson 3

Management Skills

Key Terms

management
mandatory
procrastinate
resources
visualize

What You Will Learn to Do

- Assess personal management skills

Linked Core Abilities

- Take responsibility for your actions and choices
- Apply critical thinking techniques

Skills and Knowledge You Will Gain along the Way

- Identify five management principles
- Compare management skills and leadership skills
- Define key words contained in this lesson

Chapter 6

Introduction

Good **management** is an essential tool of leaders in the performance of their duties and responsibilities. The skillful execution of basic management principles by leaders is seldom an accident. It is normally the result of clear purpose, earnest effort, and intelligent direction. This lesson defines management, introduces you to five basic management principles (planning, organizing, coordinating, directing, and controlling), and compares management to leadership.

Good management is also the sound use of the available means (or **resources**) to accomplish a task. It requires careful planning by a leader to employ those resources to achieve the desired results. Because it is rare that leaders will have everything they need or want, they must strive to succeed with what they have. As you will see, the principles of management have broad application to many leadership situations.

> ## Key Note Term
>
> **management** – the act of managing; control or direction.

> ## Key Note Term
>
> **resources** – a source of help or supply.

Management Defined

Management is the process of planning, organizing, coordinating, directing, and controlling resources such as people, material, time, and money to accomplish a mission; however, the presence of these resources does not guarantee success or mission accomplishment. How well the leader uses these resources is much more important than the fact that the resources are available.

Of all the resources available to the leader, people (or manpower) is the most important. Because leaders must use people to coordinate time, material, and money, this resource is the foundation for the use of the other three. Leaders can control and/or influence this vital resource by properly applying techniques such as the principles and factors of leadership.

We can divide the five management principles into two stages: preparation and execution. During the preparation stage, a leader must plan, organize, and coordinate. During the execution stage, a leader must direct and control. The execution stage cannot begin until after the leader has made plans, developed the necessary organization to accomplish those plans, and completed all required coordination.

Planning

Planning is the basis for the problem-solving and decision-making processes — what goes on in planning affects what is done in those two processes. Leaders spend many hours in planning the activities of their organization. They must consider what the objectives are and how they are going to accomplish them.

When planning, leaders must **visualize**, examine, consider, realize, and reflect on the factors involved in accomplishing the mission. Planning is not an easy process and it requires a lot of work. To help, there are four basic steps to planning. They are:

> ## Key Note Term
>
> **visualize** – to form a mental image.

- **Define the objective.** In this step, leaders begin to determine the tasks and conditions that are necessary to complete the objective. Timing is very important. Leaders must ensure that their team members can do all tasks within the specified time frame.

- **Study the situation.**

- **List and examine possible courses of action the leader could take.**

- **Select the course of action that will achieve the objective.**

Additionally, there are four factors that leaders must consider when using the planning process to make and implement plans.

- **Time.** Leaders must consider time as they plan events, meet deadlines, and set goals; then they make plans and execute tasks according to an established time schedule. Effective leaders will schedule their time and the activities of their team to meet these events, deadlines, and goals.

- **Effort.** Leaders must exert effort to get things done. You cannot expect results if you do not work at putting your plan into action. Successful leaders are energetic. They work hard to accomplish goals — you should exercise that same type of effort.

- **Patience.** Patience is an ingredient that all leaders must possess. It is hard to be patient when challenges occur. To solve a difficult situation, you should re-examine the facts, coordinate with people who may be helpful, and readjust the plan, if necessary. Most important, do not give up. Exercise patience and maturity while the designated people carry out the plan.

- **Objective Attitude.** An objective attitude is the ability to see and consider the different sides of an issue or situation. It involves being flexible, listening to opposing points of view, making compromises, or making changes when necessary. Your objective attitude determines how much time, effort, and patience you are willing to exert to ensure mission accomplishment.

Finally, leaders must plan or estimate approximately how many people (or man hours) they will need to accomplish the objective. Before selecting these people or defining specific tasks (done under organizing), leaders must consider the requirements of the objective against the capabilities of their team members.

Organizing

Organizing is the process of creating the conditions necessary to effectively execute your plans. It involves systematically defining the tasks and arranging the resources with respect to the achievement of your objective. There are five factors involved in organizing. They are:

- **Determine/fine-tune each task.** Identify all the tasks and subtasks that the team must do to accomplish the objective. Be specific. Develop detailed lists to record them and set measurable standards for each task/subtask.

- **Select personnel.** After you have a detailed list of tasks and subtasks, assign people to them. You should base your assignments on what each task/subtask requires versus the capabilities of your team members.

- **Develop a working structure.** With a detailed list of tasks completed and people assigned to do them, you are ready to organize the list sequentially. Determine which tasks your team must do first, second, and so on until you have included everything necessary to carry out the plan. The next step, setting priorities, goes hand-in-hand with this step. You and your teammates cannot do everything at once.

- **Set priorities.** Because some tasks are more important than others or you must start them before others because of their degree of difficulty, organize a to-do list in terms of priority for every task and subtask you have identified. Establish priorities in categories such as priority A, priority B, priority C, and so on, for each item on the to-do list. Do the A priorities first, then the Bs, the Cs, and so on.

  Allow sufficient time for each team member to do the job well. Not planning sufficient time for each task could result in the work being half-done or done "slipshod." Finally, you should develop a system for checking each other and ensuring that team members accomplish their tasks according to set standards and on time.

  A common fault among many people is that of spending too much time on tasks that are unimportant. Another fault is the tendency to **procrastinate**, or to put off those things that need to be done. When studying for an exam or doing a project, do you find yourself putting it off until the last minute? Then, you have to rush just to get the material studied or the project finished. Know what is **mandatory** and what is not when setting priorities and organizing your time.

- **Allocate resources.** In the final step of your organizing process, you must ensure that you have identified all required resources necessary for completing the objective, set aside all available resources, and planned for obtaining those that are not available.

Key Note Term

procrastinate – to put off or delay.

mandatory – something that absolutely must be done.

Coordinating

Coordinating is the active process of establishing contact and then keeping in constant touch with everyone involved to ensure the successful accomplishment of the objective. Coordination is an essential part of the planning process. Plans that are not properly coordinated cannot be properly executed, directed, or controlled.

A good rule of thumb to follow is to coordinate with everyone you think might be involved somehow or at some point in completing the objective. Through coordination, leaders secure the cooperation of people not under their direct control. A key to effective coordination is the use of friendly persuasion and mutual cooperation.

Directing

Directing is the active process by which a leader issues instructions to achieve a predetermined objective. The leader uses two common methods of directing — written or spoken. Be sure to include all the necessary details and information in your directions. In an office situation, many supervisors may decide to direct through the written word by passing out memos. After you have told everyone by written or spoken directions what is expected of them, you must supervise to ensure that they go by the rules you have laid down. There are four basic types of directing that leaders use. These are:

- **Demand.** A straightforward statement telling what must be done, who must do it, and when it must be done. For example, you tell cadets unexcused absences will not be tolerated.

- **Request.** A milder, more tactful approach to reaching the objective. The results usually would be the same if you requested, instead of demanded, specific behavior. In the Demand example, you would ask your cadets to please provide reasons for each absence.

- **Suggestion.** This type of directing is used only when a suggestion is strong enough to get the job done. It relies on the manners and good taste of those to whom you make the suggestion. Here the leader suggests what should be done but does not say, when, by whom, or how it should be done. You may suggest to cadets it is preferable to provide an authorized excuse for any absence as soon as possible.

- **Volunteer.** Leaders rarely use this method except when they want to get someone to do something that they cannot require them to do. Because volunteering means for someone to offer assistance, here you would ask your cadets who are consistently absent to schedule a counseling session to discuss any problems they are having attending class.

Controlling

Controlling is when leaders compare the tasks that their team members are actually doing to the tasks that they had directed and planned the team to do at any point in the project. Remember, you have direct control over the managerial actions of your teammates.

Then, based on your team's progress, your options may include proceeding with the way the plan is progressing, modifying the plan and continuing on with it, or stopping the action and starting over again. As the leader, it is your responsibility to ensure that the objective is met within the required standards and according to the established deadlines. Controlling is continuous until you complete the task.

Management vs. Leadership

Leadership deals with the personal relationship of one person to another. It is the way a leader influences subordinates to accomplish the mission. Management, then, is a set of activities or behaviors performed by those in senior positions to obtain, direct, or allocate resources to accomplish goals and tasks. A good leader will think and plan in a rational manner in order to efficiently utilize the talent and skills of the individuals that make up the team.

How do leadership and management relate? You must realize that although they are separate processes, you will almost never use them separately. At lower levels, you lead through face-to-face dealings with your people. You are still a manager, but higher levels of authority in the chain of command control most of the physical resources.

As leaders get promotions, they control more resources. Instead of just leading a group, they may now be responsible for the overall operation of the organization.

For example, if you were the assistant manager at a fast food restaurant, you would be behind the counter with your kitchen crew making sure they were performing their jobs correctly and in a responsible manner. If you were promoted to manager, you would not have as much face-to-face contact with the kitchen crew. Instead, you would be more concerned with putting together work schedules, hiring, and ordering food supplies and equipment. You would then check with your assistant manager to make sure that the employees were doing their jobs.

Time Management

In the reality of life, time will be one of your most valuable resources. As a leader, you must learn to use time wisely and to your best advantage.

Most everyone can benefit from timesaving techniques that will make them more efficient managers of time. The following list addresses various timesaving techniques. Keep these techniques in mind and try to incorporate as many of them as you can in your everyday life. By following these tips, you will become a more effective time manager and a better leader.

- **Goal setting is the first and foremost key to success. The key points and the importance of goal setting were covered earlier in this lesson. Try posting notes around your area that will remind you of your goals.**
- **Learn to set priorities. After you set your goals, determine your priorities. Learn to do first things first.**
- **Identify your attention span and schedule/do work accordingly.**
- **Thoroughly plan your work. In planning, learn to delegate authority. This will help so that you do not waste time and effort.**
- **Make use of your spare time.**
- **Learn to say no to yourself and others.**
- **Examine old habits that may prevent efficiency.**
- **Do not strive for absolute perfection.**
- **Learn to outline.**
- **Use a desktop or pocket diary.**
- **Use a file system.**
- **Set time limits on meetings.**

As a leader, you also need to be aware of "time wasters." Create an effective time management environment within your team — both you and your team members should learn to avoid these pitfalls. The most common time wasters include:

- **Lack of organization**
- **Lack of priorities**

- **Lack of delegation**
- **Unclear objectives**
- **No plan available and no, or little, time spent planning**
- **No coordination**
- **No teamwork**
- **Procrastination**
- **Lack of self-discipline**
- **Lack of feedback**
- **Interruptions**

These management tips will help you to become a leader who is more efficient in managing your time as well as your team.

Conclusion

Becoming a leader means learning to manage your resources — people, money, material, and time — to their fullest extent. You must also continue to search for more effective ways of improving your management techniques. Whether you use the principles of management in your everyday life or as a member of the JROTC program, you must use them to your best advantage.

People with authority have the responsibility of leading and managing. To succeed, they must exercise leadership when dealing with subordinates while at the same time properly managing the resources of their organization.

Lesson Review

1. **What is the most important resource available to a leader? Why?**
2. **List the five basic principles of management.**
3. **What are the four basic types of directing?**
4. **Choose one time waster and discuss how this affects your life.**

Chapter 6

Lesson Review

Lesson 4

Communication

Key Terms

communication
decodes
emotional intelligence
encodes
feedback
message
transference
transmitted

What You Will Learn to Do

- Adapt communication to give direction and provide feedback to others

Linked Core Abilities

- Communicate using verbal, non-verbal, visual, and written techniques
- Treat self and others with respect

Skills and Knowledge You Will Gain along the Way

- Discuss how communication is important for effective leadership
- Explain the basic flow and purpose of informal communication
- Review the major elements of a communication model
- Review how to overcome barriers of effective communication
- Define key words contained in this lesson

Introduction

It's not what you say, but what you do. This statement highlights the philosophy that actions speak louder than words. You are a model for others. They watch what you do and, if they admire you, will imitate your actions. Communicating is sending a message through a process that allows the receiver to understand the message as you intended. Many things affect this process. In this lesson, you learn about the process of communication, the barriers to that process, the power of emotional intelligence, and the process exchanging feedback.

Even though your actions speak louder than the words you use, words still influence others. To be effective, there must be an understanding of what is heard and alignment of actions with what you are saying. Effective communication is important in our lives. It is the number one cause of interpersonal conflict, and we spend over 70 percent of our waking hours communicating through some means (writing, reading, listening, speaking).

Communication is defined as the transference and understanding of a meaning. Note the two words **transference** AND understanding. It is not enough to just send a message. For the communication to be successful, it must be understood. This is no easy task.

The Communication Process

First, someone has something they want to say, a **message** to be sent. Then the sender **encodes** this message. That means the sender puts it into some symbolic form to be transmitted. After the message is encoded, it is **transmitted** through some medium. This could be written, spoken, nonverbal gestures or expressions, paper, television, audiotape, and so on. The receiver then **decodes** the message. He/she must put the message in some symbolic form that they understand. Finally, through **feedback**, the sender determines whether the message was received as intended. This is shown in Figure 6.4.1.

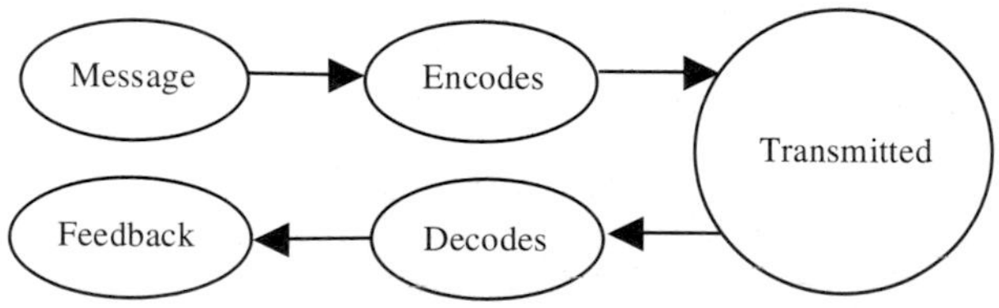

Key Note Term

communication – sharing of information.

transference – the act of transferring.

Key Note Term

message – a communication transmitted between persons by written or spoken words, signals, and so on.

encodes – converts.

transmitted – to send from one person to another.

decodes – translates.

feedback – verifying that a message was received in the manner it was intended.

Figure 6.4.1: The communication process.

Sounds easy, doesn't it? Well, it is much more complicated than that, and that is why most communication is not understood and often creates conflict. There are many hidden barriers affecting the process.

For example, the encoding and decoding process is greatly affected by the sender and receiver's skills, attitude and knowledge. His/her skills in reading, writing, listening, and reasoning influence what is said, how well it is said, and with what meaning it is sent or received. In an earlier lesson, you learned that attitudes can affect your behavior. When you are communicating, your attitude can affect the tone of your voice, the words you choose to use, and the readiness to listen. Your knowledge about the topic also has an impact on how well you can communicate about the message.

Additional barriers exist. We often filter what we say; we drop things out of the message based on what we think the listener needs to know or wants to know. We choose what to say. We listen selectively; we listen for what we want to hear. We are overloaded with information to the point of not knowing how to organize or use all this information. We might be defensive or apprehensive about the message and not want to hear what is being said. Languages, accents, and jargon affect what we hear and what we think it means. Is it any wonder we have difficulty being understood?

You will be building your skills around communication in speaking and writing techniques in other lessons. One barrier discussed in this lesson is one's emotions and how they interfere in the communication process. This can be done by understanding **emotional intelligence**.

Emotional Intelligence

Emotions are real. They create a need to "react" in a situation that faces us. When faced with a dangerous situation it is the brain quickly telling the rest of your body that something is not right and it is time to either run away or stand and fight. Emotions cannot be checked at the door and forgotten until the day is over. If you have a disagreement with your parents before school, the emotions around that disagreement are influencing your behavior the rest of the day, possibly the week. They will influence what you hear, what you say, and how you behave. They will become barriers to understanding or sending a message.

People who have a high degree of emotional intelligence have a greater degree of influence. Their behaviors reflect they are aware of what the emotion is that is present, understand why that emotion is there, and are able to separate the emotion and the reaction so they can manage the emotion rather than the emotion managing them.

There are five competencies or skills to managing your emotions: self-awareness, self-regulation, self-motivation, empathy, and effective relationships. These are covered in the following sections.

> ### Key Note Term
>
> **emotional intelligence** – the ability for one to monitor their emotions and use information about those emotions to guide one's thinking and actions.

Self-awareness

Self-awareness is the ability to "feel" the emotion and understand where it is coming from. Read the following list. What would you be feeling if you were in the following situations?

A slow line at the video store

Making a presentation in class

A surprise birthday party

Being told on Friday that you cannot go to the ballgame on Saturday

A phone call from an old friend

Different emotions can happen in similar situations. The slow line may not be a problem if you are not in a hurry; however, add to that situation that you have only a few minutes to get home on time or your parent will be grounding you for a week.

Now that you have identified the "feeling" that is going on inside you in those situations, think about the consequences those feelings might bring. For example, the slow line and your need to be home on time, could bring about your making comments to the people in front of you if they are not ready to ring up their purchase. Or it might make you moody and be abrupt with your friends who are waiting in the car for you.

The emotion will drive different "actions" or consequences. You need to know what the emotion is (fear, frustration, anger, disappointment) and why it exists (what consequences the situation might bring, therefore how you might react to the emotion).

Self-regulation

Self-regulation is the ability to control that emotion. Do not ignore or push aside the emotion, but rather recognize it and deal with it effectively. Take a pause between the emotion and your reaction to it. And more important, identify what you are telling yourself at that time — self-talk.

What you tell yourself goes immediately to your subconscious where it increases or decreases your anger or other emotions. Repeated negative self-talk leads to exaggerated and irrational thinking. Have you ever said these things to yourself?

They always take me for granted.

I'm always late.

No one ever helps me.

No one ever listens to me.

It will always be this way.

Everything I do is wrong.

I never get a passing grade.

Now think about why you say those things to yourself. For example, if you are always late, why are you late? Are you only late at certain times? Be more specific about your being late. After you have identified why you say those things to yourself, you can begin to identify the emotions around the reasons you are late which is driving the behavior to be late. It could be that you are not getting to bed early enough to get a good night sleep. It could be that you are not prepared for that class. It could be that you don't like that particular teacher. Whatever the reason, after you have identified it, you can change the self-talk from "I'm always late" to "I am late because I do not get enough sleep." The next question would be why don't I get enough sleep? Because I don't start my homework until after dinner. What can I do to start my homework earlier so I can get a good night sleep? You see it is a series of questions getting to the root of the problem, which is creating in you an emotion that is driving negative self-talk and negative behaviors.

Self-motivation

Self-motivation is the ability to change the way you think about things to get them done. There are things about our lives, school, family, and community that we don't enjoy doing. But they must be done. Learning to connect to those things in a positive way is a big part of emotional intelligence. Can you identify a few things about school that make you feel uncomfortable or bored? Now answer the next two questions: Why are these things important? How might you think about these things differently so that you can take greater satisfaction in them?

Empathy

Empathy is the ability to share your feelings with others more openly so they will open up and trust you, improving communication overall. Think of someone you are close to. Someone you tell everything to. Do you trust that person? Do they trust you? Then think of someone you tell very little to. What is your trust level with them? Each relationship will build a different trust level; however, it begins with you. The greater the trust, the more open the communication. The more open the communication the greater the trust. Kind of like the story, which came first the chicken or the egg?

The four levels of communication are shown in Table 6.4.1.

Table 6.4.1: The Four Levels of Communication

Superficial	"Hi!" "How are you doing?"
Fact	"It is raining."
Thought	"I think you are good at that."
Feeling	"I feel you don't care about your homework."

With some people, you never get past the first two levels. To open the trust and communication you will want to reach the fourth level.

Effective Relationships

Effective relationships are about what occurs from your ability to be self-aware, to self-regulate and self-motivate and to create empathy with others. It creates an enthusiasm, which is contagious. It is about finding those things you love about what you are doing and creating such an energy level around those things that dealing with those things you don't like can be easier. Earlier we thought about things you did not like about school. Now think about things you like best in school. What makes those things so appealing?

The communication process of sending and receiving a message is successful when the message is understood. Many barriers exist that get in the way of our message being understood. Your behaviors speak louder than your words. Your overall communication is increased by your ability to engage in your emotions, rather than keeping them at bay. Emotional intelligence allows you to become aware of the emotions, regulate their consequences, find ways to motivate yourself to complete tasks you may not like to do, feel empathy with others and build effective relationships — increasing the likelihood that the message sent is the message received.

Exchanging Feedback

Although feedback is seen as the final loop back to the sender, it is present throughout the process. How and when to give feedback is important to the process. Having a high degree of emotional intelligence increases the effectiveness of providing and receiving feedback.

Feedback is something you give as well as receive. Whether the gift is welcome or not depends on knowing when and how to share your reflections so that others accept, value, and seek out your point of view. When you give feedback in a caring and skillful way, you open a window on the world.

In the give and take of effective feedback, you need the skills to create a zone of safety in which honest and constructive information can be exchanged. Those who are people smart are adept at inviting others to give them constructive feedback. They are also talented at getting invited by others to give them feedback. They are able to give feedback that is constructive and enlightening.

You might have had bad experiences with feedback. Perhaps you were on the receiving end of too much criticism from people in authority (parents, teachers, supervisors), or felt put down by peers when we were most vulnerable. However, you can structure the feedback process in ways that create a sense of safety for yourself and for others.

To receive feedback you need to let others know that they want it; that they are receptive to hearing both the positive and negative story. To avoid being overburdened by too much feedback you need to be specific in your request for feedback. Specify why you want the feedback, what areas you want feedback in, and how much feedback you want. The following is one example of how to ask for feedback.

"Sarah, the more I'm learning about leadership, the more I'm coming to understand that receiving feedback is important to making me a better leader specifically, listening to others' ideas. I really want to make a difference in our unit and I want to understand how my behavior affects the team. I'd like you to help me with this by sharing your honest opinions with me. Would you be willing to do that?

"You can help me today by answering two questions. What are some things I do that make it easier for you to convey your ideas, and what is one thing I could do differently?"

Compare the previous request for feedback to this one:

"Sarah, the team leader told me I needed to get some feedback from others about my listening skills. I listen to others don't I?"

Getting feedback from only one source could lead you down the wrong corrective road. Getting the feedback and agreeing with it are two separate things. That is why you want to broaden your circle of feedback sources. Your Success Profiler is a good tool to use to receive feedback from any sources around the same questions. Also, posing the same questions to a number of people can validate what you are told. If most of the people you ask have similar input, you can assume there is some validity in their comments. Even if you are uncomfortable with it.

If you are not ready to receive feedback (or if someone else is not ready to receive your feedback) you will most likely deny, discount, or defend yourself instead of listening to it. To be invited to give feedback entails four key behaviors. You need to:

- **Ask for permission**
- **Share rather than insist**
- **Time your input**
- **Check others' perceptions**

By asking permission to share feedback, you can set the stage for your input and assess the recipient's readiness to listen. Some ways to seek permission might be:

- **Is this a good time for you to hear some feedback about...**
- **Would you be open to hearing some input about...**
- **I have some input on how you handled... Would you like to hear them?**
- **May I share some reactions with you about...**

Finding the right time and the right level of receptivity will enhance the likelihood the feedback will be heard. That is the same for you as the receiver. If it is not a good time for you to receive feedback, let them know that and agree to a better time and place.

Share your feedback in a form of a hypothesis rather than to insist that it is a fact. There might be a reason behind the behavior you were not aware of. By not insisting you are right, you help your recipient trust you and feel safe. The following is an example:

Sarah has accepted your offer to share some feedback about her presentation to the class. You had noticed that Sarah was speaking very fast and seemed to be cramming in too much information into the presentation. You ask: "I was wondering if you felt pressured to cover every aspect of the topic in your presentation?" When Sarah agrees that this was the case, you ask: "If you could only address three main points, what would they be and why?"

The timing of the feedback is essential to it being heard. Feedback is most effective when it is immediate. Old stuff is not relevant. Memories fade quickly. Whenever possible go for an instant replay while the behavior in question is fresh; however, being sensitive to the circumstances is important as well. Providing feedback in public can be embarrassing. Think through the impact that the time and setting will have so you can reduce distractions and increase the usefulness of your input.

Checking the recipient's perceptions about your feedback is a final closing point to the feedback process. Ask them how they felt about what you said, was there agreement or disagreement, was your input helpful or confusing, and/or does the person need more information? It helps to use effective listening skills such as paying attention to people's words and body language, and clarifying the meaning of their reactions. If there has been miscommunication or feelings have been hurt, often clarification can help the situation.

Feedback is most useful if it is constructive, concise, and specific. People are more open to positive feedback than negative. If you can tell them what they are doing right, they will most likely listen and repeat the behavior in the future. Informative feedback includes specific behaviors, is limited, and provides suggestions.

Global statements are not correctable. Specific behaviors are. Compare the following two statements:

Global: You have an attitude problem.

Specific: You sounded rather impatient at the team meeting today.

Behaviors can lead to some conclusions about personal values that can be misinterpreted. Be sure you avoid being personal and dig deep to find the behavior that needs to be challenged. Look at the following examples:

Personal: You are sloppy and disorganized.

Behavior: There is a lot of clutter in your locker. How do you find what you need?

Personal: You are lazy.

Behavior: You often procrastinate, don't finish the task, and return late from breaks. Why do you think you do this?

Personal: You are well organized.

Behavior: You are consistent in your prioritizing of assignments, setting deadlines and keeping materials readily available.

In each of these examples, the specific behaviors convey more information than the personal statements. People can hear the message more easily, can see the behaviors you are speaking about and are not confronted with labels that provide no direction — either good or bad.

Have you ever been confronted with a list of things you do wrong? You might start off with a high degree of listening, but after a while, it gets difficult. Keep your feedback focused on the main point.

Show your concern for the recipient's growth by suggesting ways they can build on their strengths and overcome deficits. Your suggestions should be specific, realistic, positive, and tactful.

> Example: "You often interrupt when others are speaking. When you do that to me, it makes me feel you do not value what I have to say. I think you would be a more effective team member if you practiced better listening skills. Would you be willing to work on this during the next team meeting? When you feel yourself ready to speak before the other person is finished, could you take a deep breath and hear them out? If you would like, I can sit next to you and if you begin to interrupt someone, I can gently tap your arm so you are aware of your behavior."

When you follow-up on your feedback, the recipient feels you care. In the example you just read you could continue the feedback process after the team meeting by asking:

> "I saw you really working at this today. You caught yourself the first time and stopped, apologized and took a deep breath. When I tapped your arm, you were able to sit back in your seat and let the team talk through the problem. By the end of the meeting you seemed much more comfortable in waiting your turn to speak. You also did a great job summarizing what others had said. How did it feel to you when you were able to stop yourself and let the others finish? Was it helpful to have me tap your arm? What would you like to do next?"

If you were not at the meeting you could follow up by asking them:

> "How did the meeting go? Were you able to practice your deep breathing? How did that work for you? What do you think you need to do next?"

Feedback is an important part of the communication process. Emotional intelligence is an important part of feedback. Being able to manage your emotions and to give and receive informative feedback reduces many of the barriers to effective communications.

Conclusion

Communication skills take practice, but when you understand the basics and use these skills often, you can present your message in an understandable manner and get/receive feedback in a positive way.

Chapter 6

Lesson Review

Lesson Review

1. Describe the communication process.

2. List the five competencies for managing your emotions. Do you have one at which you excel? Which one and why?

3. Why is it important to exchange feedback?

4. Define the term "emotional intelligence."

Lesson 5

Motivation

Key Terms

alleviate
complement
intangible
prejudicial

What You Will Learn to Do

- Employ motivation strategies that inspire others to achieve goals

Linked Core Abilities

- Take responsibility for your actions and choices
- Treat self and others with respect

Skills and Knowledge You Will Gain along the Way

- Identify how individual performance within a group is influenced by expectations, ability, and motivation
- Explain the 14 principles of motivation
- Define key words contained in this lesson

Chapter 6

Introduction

Leaders spend a great deal of time and effort studying the technical aspects of their jobs; however, to lead effectively, they must also know what makes people "tick." By studying human behavior, leaders learn why people act and react in certain ways. Plus, leaders who care about their subordinates and are attentive to their needs are more able to influence them in accomplishing unit goals. This lesson identifies those basic needs and it explains how they can be satisfied.

Studying human behavior helps leaders to acquire the knowledge they need to better understand themselves and those they lead.

It is important that leaders learn why human beings act and react in certain ways and to identify various types of behavior. They also must learn how to influence the behavior of subordinates so that their personal goals **complement** or reinforce the goals of management.

> ### Key Note Term
>
> **complement** –
> complete.

Leaders' Concern For Group Needs

Leaders must provide purpose and goals for the group. By selecting the best course of action to reach a goal, they provide purpose. By explaining the reasoning behind decisions and demonstrating their own enthusiasm for the task, they provide direction and assistance in accomplishing the goal. This direction should also include information on the required standards of performance.

Leaders must realize that, although they are recognized as leaders because of their position, they will not be accepted until they earn the respect and confidence of the group by satisfying its needs. Successful leaders, therefore, must be more concerned with the well-being of their people than they are with themselves. They must go out of their way to give time, energy, and counsel to help their subordinates live up to their potential. By constantly showing this level of concern to their subordinates, these leaders receive a high degree of respect and loyalty from their subordinates along with their desire to accomplish team goals.

> ### Note
>
> Unselfish leaders avoid providing for their own comfort and personal advancement at the expense of others. Leaders should place the comfort, pleasure, and recreation of subordinates before that of their own. It is difficult to respect leaders who seek their own comfort over that of their subordinates or who hoard credit for achievement made possible by subordinates. True leaders place themselves last in priority and share the dangers and hardships with their subordinates.

Motivating by Satisfying Needs

Needs form the basis for actions. They motivate people to behave in certain ways and to do certain things. Consequently, motivation is a total process that is determined by the interaction of human needs, the situation, and the combination of personal and group needs. The leader's part within this interaction is to:

- **Thoroughly understand human needs and stay directed toward satisfying them. Keep a broad point of view on human nature and motivation. Do not hold to a narrow view that people are motivated only by fear, or believe the opposite—that people are all good and will always be motivated to do the right thing. Instead, a complex array of forces can motivate people, and leaders must be open to every situation.**

- **Satisfy individual and group needs by establishing goals or tasks for individuals and groups to reach, leading to goal/task accomplishment.**

- **Understand how to motivate to obtain the behavior and conduct (confidence, competence, professionalism, and so on) needed from subordinates.**

- **Establish and maintain loyalty and teamwork within the unit.**

- **Create a caring climate within the unit—one that promotes trust and respect as well as an understanding and acceptance of the "why" of subordinates' actions.**

- **Create self-motivation in subordinates—this is the most powerful and lasting form of motivation. Most people can become self-motivated if taught leadership attributes.**

14 Principles Of Motivation

Although there is no simple formula for motivation, you can understand a basic view of what motivates people. Keep in mind that this view is a simplification for you to use as a guide. It assumes that needs motivate people and that a person's motivation to reach a goal depends on whether the person perceives that the goal will satisfy any of those needs. Realizing that different people react to varying needs will allow you to arrive at appropriate decisions and actions in a particular situation.

People are motivated by many forces—values, self-interest, kindness, worthy causes, and other forces. Some of these forces are internal—such as fears and beliefs; and some are external—such as danger, the environment, a chance for promotion, or pressures from a senior, subordinates, or one's family. Forces combine to determine what a person is motivated to do in a given situation.

Because needs form the basis for actions and leaders must motivate by understanding these needs, leaders must understand how needs drive individuals, people, or groups to action. The following is a discussion of 14 practical principles (guidelines) that flow from this basic view of motivation.

> **Note**
>
> Do not confuse these principles with the 11 leadership principles.

Principle 1

Make the needs of subordinates coincide with unit tasks and missions.

Subordinates will have a natural desire to work to satisfy their own needs. When leaders link these interests and needs with those of the group, they have a powerful way to motivate.

Principle 2

Reward individual and team behavior that supports unit tasks and missions.

The opportunity to win a reward is a sound motivator. A ribbon, a medal, a certificate, or a letter are only small tangible objects, but they mean a great deal to someone psychologically. These rewards have motivating power because they are a way of satisfying social and higher needs. Awards symbolize a proud achievement. After the higher needs are awakened by such rewards, the motivation to keep working for more recognition normally increases.

Rewards can also include a simple "well done" or a "pat on the back," a promotion, or a favorable evaluation.

Principle 3

Counsel subordinates who behave in a way that is counter to unit tasks, missions, and standards.

The previous two examples were the "carrot" or the reward approach. This principle is the opposite; it is the "stick." Use this principle only when it is necessary to motivate people who do not respond to positive motivation. Before resorting to this approach; however, be certain that the task, mission, or standard was clearly communicated prior to the infraction.

Every leader in the chain of command must be involved in the discipline of the organization. This shows subordinates that even their immediate supervisor has the power of "the stick." Each case requiring counseling or disciplinary action also provides an opportunity to teach subordinate leaders how to counsel and take disciplinary action. Remember: conduct reprimands, counseling sessions, and other corrective actions as privately and as quickly as possible after an infraction. Do not humiliate or embarrass someone in front of others.

Principle 4

Set the example in all things.

If leaders show their subordinates how to act, they are teaching them at the same time. If leaders follow regulations and unit operating procedures, they are demonstrating the expected policies to be followed. By doing these actions, leaders are also proving their own degree of self-discipline.

A word of caution is in order here. No one is superhuman, and subordinates do not expect that. While they want leaders to set the example in all things and to share hardships with them, they do not want their leaders to take unnecessary risks. If they see leaders taking unnecessary risks, they may lose confidence in their judgment, affecting the morale, cohesion, and discipline of the unit.

Principle 5

Develop morale and esprit within the unit.

Morale is the mental, emotional, and spiritual state of an individual. It is how a person feels—happy, hopeful, confident, appreciated, worthless, sad, unrecognized, or depressed. Morale has a tremendous impact on motivation. High morale strengthens courage, energy, and the will to get things done. Because everything a leader does affects morale in one way or another, a leader must always be aware of how his or her actions and decisions affect it. Give subordinates something to hope for, because hope builds morale.

Esprit means team spirit—it is the spirit, soul, and state of mind of the unit. It is a product of cohesion; the overall consciousness of the unit that the subordinate identifies with and feels a part of.

Principle 6

Give subordinates tough problems, and challenge them to wrestle with them.

Coach subordinates on their problem-solving, decision-making, planning, and implementing skills. This principle:

- **Encourages (by teaching and coaching) the development of junior leaders.**
- **Motivates people who must carry out the plan.**
- **Makes communication clearer—giving everyone a better understanding of the mission and what they must do as individuals and as a team to achieve it.**
- **Creates an open, trusting communication bond between the members of the chain of command.**

Principle 7

Have subordinates participate in the planning of upcoming events.

Participating in the planning of future events can be a highly motivating experience. By contributing ideas to a plan, subordinates then have a personal interest in seeing the plan succeed. Plus, it improves communication, which improves teamwork. Improved communication also gives everyone a clearer picture of the objective so that they can use their initiative to achieve it. Clear understanding of the mission and the plan prevents ill-founded rumors and fears based on a lack of knowledge.

Also, by involving subordinates in planning, leaders show that they recognize subordinates' abilities and appreciate them. Recognition and appreciation from respected leaders are powerful motivating forces.

Principle 8

Alleviate causes of the personal concerns of subordinates so that they can concentrate on their jobs.

Everyone has a unique combination of experience, values, character traits, knowledge, and skills, causing a person to have a unique way of dealing with life. Things that seem of no importance to leaders may be of critical importance to subordinates.

Some people may have family problems that leaders must empathize with before they can help them. Others may not know how to handle money, have meaningful relationships, stay out of trouble, balance the demands of school or work with the needs of the family, or grow professionally and personally.

Leaders should strive to help their subordinates as much as they can by keeping them informed of situations and decisions, encouraging feedback, and through counseling—when necessary. For those people who are having real or perceived challenges, these difficulties will cause them to worry, consume their energy, and prevent them from being productive. To help **alleviate** these causes of personal concerns, leaders should teach subordinates how to handle their lives in a healthy, constructive way.

Principle 9

Ensure that subordinates are properly cared for and have the tools they need to succeed.

Simply put, this principle means caring for subordinates. Leaders at all levels of the chain of command must do all they can to help subordinates meet their physical, safety, social, esteem, and self-fulfillment needs. Teach them all you know. You want them to have the right values, character traits, knowledge, and skills because these are the tools that will allow them to grow, and to live happy, productive lives.

Principle 10

Keep subordinates informed about missions and standards.

Keep clear, open communications with subordinates so that they can accomplish their mission as a team and use initiative in the absence of orders.

Principle 11

Use positive peer pressure to work for you, the leader, and the unit.

Peer pressure can be a powerful motivating force, but leaders must be careful how they apply it. If not used properly, it can backfire with serious consequences. On the other hand, positive peer pressure that is based on professional norms and values is healthy.

Key Note Term

alleviate – to relieve.

Principle 12

Avoid using statistics as a major method of evaluating units and motivating subordinates.

Statistics in themselves are not necessarily bad or good. Leaders should use them sparingly and carefully because they are only the "mask" of a unit and they may present a false image. They are surface indicators or symptoms that leaders need to check into further. Perhaps they indicate a serious problem; perhaps not. Leaders simply do not know until they look into the true causes of the symptoms.

Improper use of statistics has a devastating effect on trust, morale, and motivation. Valid evaluation systems and effective leaders require much more than statistics. They require ways to get beneath the "image" to the real substance—the true strengths and weaknesses that influence effectiveness and the real leadership causes of those strengths and weaknesses. Good leaders make the time to get out and to see the real substance of a unit.

Principle 13

Make the jobs of subordinates as challenging, exciting, and meaningful as possible.

Make each subordinate feel special. Experience and study have proven that people need meaningful work. They need to believe that what they are doing, even if it is tiring and unpleasant, is necessary and important. When people feel that their jobs are important and that they have responsibility, they feel needed and motivated. This principle encourages the delegation of authority. This "power down" approach helps leaders get the best out of their subordinates. Leaders give responsibility to subordinates who have the skill and will to handle it, and they strive to make subordinates feel that they are as responsible as them for achieving unit standards and goals.

Principle 14

Do not tolerate any form of prejudicial talk or behavior.

Racial, sexual, or other **prejudicial** talk and behavior are contrary to the principles on which America was founded. If a person feels that he or she is the object of prejudice, that person's motivation can be seriously damaged. Prejudice can also destroy teamwork, cohesion, and discipline within a unit.

Although these 14 principles of motivation are different from the 11 leadership principles, there are similarities. Did you recognize any?

Key Note Term

prejudicial – to form an opinion without knowing or in spite of the facts.

Building Motivation

People will have little motivation to do something if they believe they cannot succeed. Likewise, if they are not convinced that good performance is the best way to satisfy their needs, their motivation will be low and they will have little or no interest in doing their best. However, when subordinates are convinced that their chances for success are good enough to warrant the effort, this belief will help them to achieve their own goals (or needs) as well as those of the group. Therefore, leaders must know their subordinates' capabilities, establish challenging goals within those capabilities, and employ them in accordance with those capabilities (one of the leadership principles). Leaders can also build confidence by offering support, encouragement, and assistance.

Creating assurance that good performance will be rewarded is based on three factors:

- **The leader has a consistent record of checking and evaluating performance.**
- **The leader has an equally consistent record of using rewards in respect to improving performance.**
- **The leader knows that some team players feel that completion of the task itself is sufficient reward.**

Tangible and Intangible Rewards

People work for the opportunity to receive tangible (a plaque) or **intangible** (a "pat on the back") rewards, and the need to believe that their work is necessary and important. If supervisors never compliment them on a job well done, however, it is easy for subordinates to feel that they never do good work or that their leaders are not interested in their work. Either of these beliefs can destroy motivation.

On the other hand, if leaders recognize and confirm each person's importance and value to the organization, motivation will be strong. Highly motivated teams with high morale usually have leaders who take a personal interest in them and are understanding.

People resent a lack of respect and will respond with that same disrespect by doing only what is necessary to get by. Leaders must build bonds of mutual respect, trust, confidence, and understanding that are fundamental to a disciplined, cohesive team.

> **Key Note Term**
>
> **intangible** – that which has a value not dependent of physical makeup.

Conclusion

This lesson explained one of the most important aspects that you, as a leader, must KNOW to DO your job properly—the understanding of human nature and how that understanding impacts on what you must KNOW about yourself, your job, your subordinates, and your unit. This knowledge will give you a stronger foundation for what you must BE and what you must DO; then, what you do as a leader—the application of these skills—flows from this "being" and "knowing" foundation.

Invisible threads weave together many of the techniques and attributes of leadership. This lesson illustrated how understanding needs is intertwined with a leader's values, ethics, and character and with various leadership traits and principles. Your knowledge and proper application of human nature is essential—it is the bedrock of your character as a leader.

Lesson Review

1. Compare and contrast tangible and intangible rewards.
2. How do the 14 principles of motivation compare to the 11 principles of leadership? What are the similarities? What are the differences?
3. Choose one of the 14 principles of motivation and explain it.
4. Why is it important to establish and maintain loyalty and teamwork within the unit?

Unit 3

Foundations for Success

NEFE High School Financial Planning Program

Chapter 11

Lesson 5

Credit: Buy Now, Pay Later

Chapter 11

Key Terms

annual fee
annual percentage rate (APR)
bankruptcy
credit
credit history
credit report
debt
finance charge
grace period
interest
loan term

What You Will Learn to Do

- Appraise personal credit worthiness

Linked Core Abilities

- Take responsibility for your actions and choices

Skills and Knowledge You Will Gain along the Way

- Identify the advantages of using credit
- Identify the various costs related to credit
- Compare common sources for building credit
- Discuss the factors to consider to establish credit
- Define key words contained in this lesson

Introduction

Think of a time you borrowed money from a friend or family member. Were you able to build a good borrowing reputation by promptly repaying the money? Were the terms to repay the money fair? When you are in a situation when you need to make a large purchase such as a car, you might need to borrow money from a bank or other financial business. To use this type of credit wisely and avoid problems, you need to know what is involved. In this learning plan you explore ways to use credit. You also consider your rights and responsibilities of using credit.

Note

You will find this lesson in your NEFE High School Financial Planning Program Student Guide

For more information go to *www.nefe.org* or write to

NEFE High School Financial Planning Program

5299 DTC Blvd., Suite 1300

Greenwood Village, CO 80111

Lesson 6

Insurance: Your Protection

Key Terms

deductible
insurance
insurance premium
risk management

What You Will Learn to Do

- Relate insurance to current and future personal needs

Linked Core Abilities

- Take responsibility for your actions and choices

Skills and Knowledge You Will Gain along the Way

- Describe how insurance works
- Identify general types of insurance, including health, property, life, disability, and liability
- Discuss the costs associated with insurance coverage
- Define key words contained in this lesson

Chapter 11

Introduction

Have you ever been injured, in an accident, or had property damaged? Chances are, someone had to pay for those unexpected medical bills or costs for repairs. People use insurance as a way to protect themselves from unexpected losses. In this learning plan you will explore how different types of insurance protect you from losses. You will also uncover strategies to handle financial risk and ways to lower insurance costs.

> **Note**
>
> You will find this lesson in your NEFE High School Financial Planning Program Student Guide

For more information go to *www.nefe.org* or write to

NEFE High School Financial Planning Program

5299 DTC Blvd., Suite 1300

Greenwood Village, CO 80111

Chapter 12

Teaching Skills

Lesson 1

Preparing to Teach

Key Terms

competency
learning objectives
learning outcomes
lesson plans
measurable
prerequisite
training aids

What You Will Learn to Do

- Prepare to teach

Linked Core Abilities

- Communicate using verbal, non-verbal, visual, and written techniques

Skills and Knowledge You Will Gain along the Way

- Describe five critical elements you need to consider in preparing to teach
- Write effective **learning outcomes**
- Describe at least six tips for planning a lesson
- Define key words contained in this lesson

Introduction

Being an instructor, or an assistant instructor, will be a challenging experience for you. It is for anyone – even experienced teachers. Teaching is also a rewarding experience because you will have the opportunity to help younger cadets learn the skills they need to succeed. As an added bonus, you will find that when you teach, you learn more about the competency and content.

In this lesson, you will consider five critical elements that are important to your success when you teach:

- **Motivation**
- **Learning Outcomes**
- **Training aids**
- **Lesson plans**
- **Knowing the Content**

Motivation

To effectively teach a class, you must be motivated. Motivation is a drive that comes from within you. When you get excited about doing something, you will discover that you have the necessary motivation to do that task well; however, the opposite is also true. If you do not get excited about the task, you will lack the necessary motivation and drive to perform the task successfully. In teaching, just doing an okay or a satisfactory job is not enough. When your instructors give you the opportunity to become a student instructor, consider it a challenging and exciting opportunity to give students in your class the solid education they deserve.

Learning Outcomes

As a student instructor, your primary responsibility is to help students achieve the **learning outcomes** for the lesson your instructor has assigned you to teach. The learning outcomes for a lesson describe what students should know and be able to do when they successfully complete the lesson.

Each JROTC lesson also includes performance standards that describe how students and the instructor will know when they are succeeding, learning activities that explain how students will achieve the learning outcomes, and assessment activities that tell how students will demonstrate their learning.

Competencies and Learning Objectives

As you prepare to teach a lesson, you will need to focus on two types of learning outcomes: *competencies* and *learning objectives*.

Key Note Term

learning outcomes – describe what students should know and be able to do as the result of a learning experience.

- A competency describes the major skill or task addressed in the lesson. Each lesson targets one competency.

- Learning objectives describe the supporting knowledge and skills needed to perform a specific competency. Learning objectives break the competency into smaller pieces that make learning easier and provide benchmarks by which students and instructors can measure progress toward achieving the lesson competency. Each lesson targets several learning objectives.

Example:

Competency	Apply mediation techniques to resolve conflict
Learning Objectives	a. Differentiate between arbitration and mediation
	b. Describe the role of a mediator and the qualities required to fulfill that role
	c. Establish ground-rules for the mediation process
	d. Facilitate the steps in the mediation process
	e. Adapt active listening skills to the mediation process
	f. Define key words: arbitration, empathy, mediation, facilitate

All learning objectives must be realistic, attainable, observable, and **measurable**. At the end of each period of instruction, you should be able to administer a test based on the criteria of the objective and on the material you presented. Likewise, students should be able to pass a test, or at least demonstrate to the best of their ability, that they have a basic understanding of the material you presented.

Note

The process to develop learning objectives is by far more complex and detailed than presented here; however, this material should give you an appreciation for what learning objectives are and the basic development procedures.

Writing Competency and Learning Objective Statements

Both competencies and learning objectives begin with one measurable action verb. Action verbs require students to <u>do</u> something: create a product, make a decision, solve a problem, or perform a task. Verbs such as "understand," "learn," and "know" are <u>not</u> action verbs and therefore <u>should not be used</u> in a competency or learning objective.

Table 12.1.1 shows examples of measurable action verbs. Refer to this list as you learn to write competencies and learning objectives in this lesson

Competencies and learning objectives are written in the same manner:

1. Write a simple, one-sentence statement that describes the skill that students will learn to do in the lesson.

Key Note Term

competency – a major skill or task that describes what a learner will be able to do as a result of a specific lesson.

Key Note Term

learning objective – a supporting skill, knowledge, or attitude leading to mastery of a competency.

Key Note Term

measurable – able to be observed and evaluated for quality.

2. Begin the statement with an action verb.

3. Add the content, object, or performance.

4. Add descriptive words.

5. Check to be sure that the competency and learning objectives are **observable** (you can see the product or watch the performance) and **measurable** (you can evaluate the quality).

Action Verb	Object	Descriptive Phrase
Apply	mediation techniques	to resolve conflict

Note

The process of developing learning outcomes is far more complex and detailed than presented here; however, this material should give you an appreciation for what learning outcomes are and the basic developmental procedures.

Table 12.1.1: Sample Action Verb List

act	discuss	predict
answer	distinguish	prepare
apply	estimate	produce
arrange	explain	rate
build	give examples of	record
calculate	identify	reply
change	illustrate	report
choose	join	restate
classify	judge	revise
compare	justify	schedule
compete	list	select
compose	match	show
compute	measure	solve
contrast	modify	state
create	name	summarize
define	organize	use
demonstrate	outline	verify
describe	perform	write/rewrite

Training Aids

Training aids are materials and tools that help students learn and help you teach. Training aids include delivery tools such as computers, overhead projectors, television sets with videocassette recorders, and chalkboards, as shown in Figure 12.1.2. They also include items that present content such as PowerPoint presentations, posters, handouts, worksheets, and so on.

To make a training aid effective, you must use it properly. Use training aids as part of your lesson; however, your entire lesson cannot rely on the use of training aids.

When you find a training aid that you like, rehearse your lesson with it. The following pointers will enable you to use training aids effectively:

- **A training aid should adequately support the material in your lesson. Clearly explain how the training aid relates to the lesson learning outcomes and content.**
- **Do not talk to your training aids. Keep your eye contact with your class as much as possible.**
- **Make your training aids are large enough for everyone to see, and if the training aids use sound, loud enough for everyone to hear.**

Key Note Term

training aids – materials such as computers, handouts, chalkboards, and so on that enhance and support teaching.

Figure 12.1.2: The chalkboard can be an effective training aid if used properly.
Courtesy of US Army JROTC.

Lesson Plans

A well-designed lesson plan is your guide for teaching an effective lesson that is accomplished within the allotted timeframe. Without a lesson plan, it would be very difficult to ensure that the students achieve the competency and learning objectives and that you teach in an organized manner. Prior to teaching, be sure to carefully review the lesson plan and the information included in the related student learning plan such as the competencies, learning objectives, performance standards, learning activities, and assessment activities. In the next lesson, you will learn how to develop and use lesson plans.

Key Note Term

lesson plan – an organized, well-written plan for how an instructor will facilitate student learning

Knowing the Content

As you review the learning plan prior to teaching, make sure that you know the content. (See Figure 12.1.2.) You must be prepared to explain concepts, answer questions, provide demonstrations of required skills, and facilitate the designated learning activities. Be sure to practice presenting information, giving instructions, and providing demonstrations prior to class. Finally, use the eight tips for preparing to teach to make sure that you are ready to teach each lesson effectively.

Figure 12.1.2: You must prepare for the lessons you will teach.
Courtesy of Phyllis Picardi/Stock Boston.

Eight Tips for Teaching

When teaching a class, use these eight tips to prepare to teach effectively. These tips will help you to capture the attention of your class, keep their attention throughout the class period, build their respect in your ability as a teacher, and ensure that they meet the intended learning outcomes of the lesson:

- **Use an opening that will grab the attention of the class.**

- **Practice the material that you plan to present to the class. Pay close attention to your pace. Know how long each section of your lesson will take. (See Figure 12.1.3.)**

- **Inform the students of the learning outcomes (competencies and learning objectives) for the lesson and your expectations.**

- **Briefly review any material from previous lessons (prerequisites) that relates to the material you are teaching.**

- **Inform or advise the students of any precautions, safety requirements, or special instructions regarding the lesson.**

- **Present the material according to your lesson plan. Use your training aids effectively. Describe any assignments or practical exercises you plan to give and ensure the class knows how to accomplish them.**

- **Use demonstration and practice activities, when appropriate, to reinforce your instruction. Give your class examples that will help them understand and complete their assignments.**

Key Note Term

prerequisite – required before moving to the next step, level, class, and so on.

- Conclude by reviewing the main points of the lesson by referring back to the learning outcomes for the lesson. Allow time for questions. That is one way to determine how well the class understood the material. If possible, review any information that the class did not fully understand. You may wish to make a list of supplemental material students can review OR set aside time to work individually with students.

Figure 12.1.3: Friends can provide valuable insight into your lesson during rehearsals.
Courtesy of Mark Richards/ PhotoEdit.

Conclusion

When conducting a class or assisting someone else to teach, proper preparation is essential to do your best. Create strong learning outcomes, develop a lesson plan, learn the content, identify the training aids you will use, and motivate yourself.

Classes have a set time period and your job is to effectively complete the lesson within that time. Remember your job is to *help* the students learn; not to learn for them. Encourage your students to share the responsibility for learning by actively engaging them in the process. If you are well-organized, well-prepared, and interested in the content, you will put yourself and your class at ease and make learning enjoyable for all of you.

Chapter 12

Lesson Review

Lesson Review

1. What are the five critical elements you need to consider while preparing to teach?

2. What are the two types of lesson learning outcomes?

3. What might be the outcome if you didn't develop a well-written and organized lesson plan?

4. What training aid do you find to be the most effective and easiest to use as an instructor and student?

Lesson 2

Using and Developing Lesson Plans

Key Terms

apply
energizer
facilitator
focus
gather
inquire
process
reflection

What You Will Learn to Do

• Develop a lesson plan

Linked Core Abilities

• Build your capacity for life-long learning
• Communicate using verbal, non-verbal, visual, and written technique

Skills and Knowledge You Will Gain along the Way

• Explain the purpose of a lesson plan
• Describe the four-phases of a lesson plan
• Relate teaching and learning to the four phase lesson plan model
• Relate learning activities to learning objectives
• Associate active learning principles to effective lesson plan development
• Define key words

Chapter 12

Introduction

During your life, both in school and out, you may be called upon to teach others about a content area in which you have some expertise. As a JROTC cadet, you may be asked to teach some aspects of the JROTC curriculum to other cadets. In order to be prepared for these situations, it is helpful to know how to plan and execute a lesson.

Lesson plans are essential tools for teaching. Instructors use a lesson plan to organize the information and activities they plan to use in class. In some cases, lesson plans help to standardize how competencies and learning objectives are taught by a large number of teachers to ensure that all students meet the same standards for performance. In these cases, the lesson plan would show teachers:

- **What students need to learn**
- **What material they should teach**
- **To what extent they should teach the material**
- **In what sequence they should teach the material**
- **What strategies and learning materials they may use to teach**

Lesson Plans

JROTC lesson plans identify the target competency and learning objectives for each lesson. They provide detailed guidelines for facilitating cadet learning activities. The lesson plans should be used in conjunction with student learning plans as tools for planning, guiding, and assessing learning. The lessons incorporate sound learning principles such as multiple intelligences, the Four-Phase Lesson Plan, brain-based learning techniques, reflection, and authentic assessment.

Learning Plans

JROTC learning plans are designed to support cadet learning. Learning plans are written for cadets. They answer the questions cadets need to know about what they will learn including the target learning outcomes (competencies and learning objectives), the criteria for performance, and the activities and assignments they will need to complete in order to learn, practice, and perform the competency. Learning plans guide cadets through the learning activities and assessment activities included in the lesson plan and help cadets take responsibility for their own learning.

To be used most effectively, cadets should have the learning plan for each lesson at the beginning of class. Engaging in a review of the learning plan at the start of each lesson, instructors or cadet leaders should:

Comparing Lesson Plans and Student Learning Plans

Double-Bubble Map - ThinkingMaps®

- **Highlight the target competency, performance standards, and learning objectives**

- **Explain why that information is important; for example, criteria tell learners how they will be evaluated on their performance**

- **Show cadets how learning plans can help them keep track of the activities they need to complete**

- **Guide cadets to refer to and use the learning plan throughout the learning process**

The Four-Phase Lesson Plan

JROTC lesson plans consist of four phases: Inquire, Gather, Process, and Apply. The following sections examine these phases in more detail:

Inquire Phase

The purpose of the **inquire** phase is to motivate and engage the students, helping them connect new learning to past experience. During the inquire phase you will also refine the lesson starting point by examining what your students already know and can do. Activities in the Inquire phase can help to answer these questions:

- **What do students know?**
- **What don't students know?**
- **What misunderstandings do students have?**
- **What are past experiences do they bring to the lesson?**
- **What do students want to know?**
- **What is the purpose of the lesson?**
- **How motivated are the students to learn the content?**
- **What are some practical reasons for students to participate in the lesson?**

During this phase you may want to use an icebreaker or **energizer** in your lesson. These are physically active games or other activities that motivate and engage learners and introduce the lesson topic.

Gather Phase

After you determine the lesson's starting point, you are ready to help your students **gather** information about what they need to know about the subject matter. You want students to acquire important facts and concepts so they may develop a better understanding and build their skills.

The purpose of the gather phase is to research and collect information from a variety of sources, to synthesize information, to evaluate existing information, to collect data, to evaluate ideas, or to observe new skills. Some important questions you can ask during this phase are:

- **How can you help students think through the concepts they need to understand?**
- **How can students actively engage in collecting the information they need to learn?**
- **How do the new concepts and ideas connect with what they already know and can do?**
- **What can students do to make sense of the new information?**
- **What new understandings can students construct?**

Process Phase

The third phase is called the **process** phase. The purpose of this phase is to use new information, process new ideas, and practice new skills. The following questions can help your students during the process phase:

- **How can students explore concepts through a variety of learning activities that support multiple intelligences?**

Key Note Terms

energizer – a learning activity designed to motivate and engage learners.

gather – the phase in a lesson plan designed to assist learners in gathering new ideas and information.

Key Note Term

process – the phase in a lesson plan designed to provide opportunities for practicing new skills and processing information.

- What ways can students show relationships among the data or concepts?

- What can students do to reinforce their understanding of the new concept?

- How can students practice and improve their ability to apply the new knowledge and skills?

- What feedback will help students improve their competence?

Apply Phase

The purpose of the **apply** phase is to help students make real-life applications of the new information or ideas. Students can consider ways to integrate the lesson concepts or skills with other curriculum areas. They can also plan ways to transfer their learning into personal use outside the classroom. Questions that can help both the instructor and students during this phase are:

- What else can be done with the information?
- What else is needed to make the information usable?
- How can students demonstrate their ability to apply their new knowledge and skills in ways that are different from those experienced in the lesson?
- How can students demonstrate their ability to apply their new competence in their lives?

Key Note Term

apply – the phase in a lesson plan designed to provide opportunities for students to demonstrate their competence and expand their ability to use it in their lives.

The Three Components of Each Phase

There are three components that are common to each of the four phases in the lesson plan. They are Direct Student Focus, Learning Activity, and Reflection.

Direct Student Focus

As a teacher, you have a responsibility to help your students **focus** on specific elements of the learning activity. You will guide their thought processes and help them focus on key processes or content during the learning activity. You will eliminate or filter extraneous information so students can direct their attention to what is critical for their learning.

For example, if the students watch a video, you will identify specific elements of the video on which to focus; if you have the students read a chapter in a book, you could list the details you expect them to extract from their reading; if the students do research on the Web, you can help clarify the research topics or important information needed from the research; and so on.

The competency and learning objectives presented in the student learning plans serve as excellent tools for directing student focus. By teaching students to refer to them and referencing them for your students as you teach, you will go a long way toward directing student focus.

Key Note Term

focus – a center of activity, attraction or attention; a point of concentration; directed attention.

Learning Activities

A learning activity is an activity designed to help students learn to perform the competency. As a teacher, you should plan activities that best present the information and allow students the opportunity to participate in the learning process. (See Figure 12.2.1.) Learning activities should relate to the learning objectives for each competency and engage students in active learning experiences for each phase of the lesson plan.

Learning activities in the **inquire** phase should set the stage for learning by capturing the students' interest and helping them connect with what they will learn. As the instructor, your primary role in the **inquire** phase is consultant. As the consultant in this phase, your job is to inspire the students to learn and to assess what the students know and what they need to learn to achieve the competency.

Figure 12.2.1: Teaching is more than just writing on a board in front of a class. Courtesy of Len Rubenstein/ Index Stock Imagery.

Typical learning activities that are effective in the inquire phase include:

- **Agree/disagree worksheets**
- **Graphic Organizers and Thinking Maps®**
- **Analogies or metaphors**
- **Pre-quizzes or pre-tests**
- **"Group" graph or "4-corners"**
- **Panel discussions**
- **Debates**
- **Homework reviews**
- **Other**

In the **gather** phase, learning activities are designed to help students obtain information from you, fellow classmates, and the learning materials. The instructor's primary role in the **gather** phase is that of presenter and resource person. As the presenter, you present information; you also serve as a resource – directing students to information, coordinating student activities, observing their progress, and answering student questions.

Typical learning activities that are effective in the gather phase include:

- **Graphic organizers and Thinking Maps®**
- **Computer searches**
- **Jigsaw**
- **Interviewing experts**
- **Demonstrations**
- **Generating examples**

- Socratic questioning
- Constructivist questions
- Field trips
- Other

In the **process** phase, learning activities should provide opportunities for students to practice new skills and help students evaluate the importance and usefulness of what they are learning. (See Figure 12.2.2.) Students also have an opportunity to check their grasp of the lesson material. Your primary role in the **process** phase is **facilitator**. As the **facilitator**, you serve as a guide or coach, coordinating student activities, observing performance, providing feedback, and answering student questions.

Typical learning activities that are effective in the process phase include:

- Games
- Laboratory experiments
- Role Play
- Peer teaching
- Rehearsal
- Simulations
- Reciprocal teaching
- Graphic organizers and Thinking Maps®
- Interviews
- Student designed homework activities
- Other

Key Note Term

facilitator – one who leads a discussion or guides an activity.

Figure 12.2.2: Practical application and field trips are very effective in the learning process.
Courtesy of Paul Mozell/ Stock Boston.

Learning activities designed for the **Apply** phase, engage students in active learning experiences that help them transfer the new information or skills outside the classroom and demonstrate their mastery of the competency. In this phase your primary role is that of mediator. As the mediator, you serve as a mentor, helping students to consider ways that the new knowledge and skills can be applied to their everyday lives and how it connects to what they are learning in other classes. You also provide feedback as students complete assessments that require them to demonstrate their competence. As the mentor, this is your opportunity to encourage students to make improvements in their performance when needed, and most importantly, to celebrate their successes!

Typical learning activities that are effective in the apply phase include:

- Action research
- Portfolios
- Personal goals and objectives

- Creative connections
- Problem-based projects
- Demonstration of competence
- Peer and instructor review of products and performance
- Self evaluation of learning and developed or expanded competence
- Other

Reflection

The **reflection** process is important because it causes students think about the importance and purpose of what they are learning and to see how the learning activity has helped them learn. Reflecting also helps the brain store information into long-term memory.

As the teacher, ask questions that help students think about, reflect on, or make sense of their learning experiences. Having students discuss or write down what they understand helps them clarify their thinking and improve their understanding, as well as strengthen their memory connections.

The Four–Phase Lesson Plan is based on a learning model in which lecture and reading is minimized, and in which group discussion, learning by doing, and teaching others are emphasized. In each of the four phases, students reflect on what they have learned, how they have learned it, and what they are going to do with it.

Conclusion

For teachers, lesson plans provide the map or blueprint for teaching and facilitating a well-designed lesson. The Four-Phase Lesson Plan facilitates the planning and teaching processes. As you develop each phase of your lesson plan, remember to include activities that address the following components: Direct Student Focus, Learning Activities, and Reflection.

Be sure to provide learning plans for your students. Learning plans help your students take responsibility for their own learning by guiding them through the learning process and answering the following questions:

Why is this important?

What will I learn?

How will I demonstrate that I have learned?

What strategies will help me learn?

If you are called upon to teach a lesson, your students will benefit from this well-organized approach.

Lesson Review

1. List the four lesson plan phases. Choose one and explain it.
2. What are the three components to each lesson plan phase?
3. Define the term "facilitator" and explain what a facilitator does.
4. What should a standardized lesson plan reflect?

Delivering Instruction

Key Terms

brainstorming
case study
coach-pupil exercises
conference
demonstration
discussion
gaming
group performance
independent exercise
lecture
practical exercise
role-playing
team practical exercises

What You Will Learn to Do

- Use effective teaching methods to deliver instruction

Linked Core Abilities

- Communicate using verbal, non-verbal, visual, and written techniques

Skills and Knowledge You Will Gain along the Way

- Compare lesson objectives to learning objectives
- Distinguish among the seven teaching methods
- Identify the five types of practice exercises
- Define key words

Introduction

From time-to-time, you may be required to present a portion of the course content. When this occurs, you will need to know some of the finer points necessary to teach that instruction.

Recall that in the "Preparing to Teach" lesson, you learned how to prepare yourself to teach, develop learning objectives (consisting of tasks, conditions, and standards), and use training aids. In the "Using and Developing Lesson Plans" lesson, you learned how to develop four-phase lesson plans (Inquire, Gather, Process, Apply). You may want to review all or a portion of that material before proceeding with this lesson.

In this lesson you learn different teaching methods and when to use each method, such as demonstration and lecture, five practical exercise formats, and the rehearsal process.

Types of Teaching Methods

The method of instruction is how you choose to conduct your class. Sometimes, the subject you are teaching dictates which method to use. There are many different types of instruction from which to choose. The following sections give you some ideas about different methods of instruction.

Lecture

The **lecture** is an informative talk given to a class. During a lecture, the teacher does most of the talking; questions and answers usually occur at the end of the lecture. Because the teacher limits the interaction during the presentation, this method provides the fastest dissemination of information.

Use lectures when the subject you are teaching is unfamiliar to your class and it is the best method for preparing students to practice the task. Generally, this method involves learning knowledge-based information. Knowledge-based information is that which you need to know or understand. Examples of JROTC subjects for which you might use a lecture are History, Citizenship, or Technology Awareness.

When preparing for a lecture, be sure to research your topic, organize your thoughts using the outline of the lesson plan, and rehearse. Remember to use your training aids while practicing. Ensure that you are comfortable with your topic because you will be doing most of the talking.

The question and answer session at the end of the lecture gives your class the opportunity to ask for clarification or additional information, and it gives you the opportunity to reemphasize the lesson learning objectives.

> **Key Note Term**
>
> **lecture** – teaching method designed to provide instruction on a task or topic.

Key Note Term

conference – a teaching method where the instructor involves the entire class in a discussion of the subject being taught by asking leading questions to get the students to think about and discuss the main points.

discussion – a teaching method where the instructor involves the entire class in a discussion of the subject by asking leading questions to get the students to think about and discuss the main points.

demonstration – a teaching method that requires hands-on class participation.

practical exercise – a maneuver, operation, or drill carried out for training a discipline.

Discussion/Conference

There are two names for this method of teaching. During a **conference**, the instructor involves the entire class in a **discussion** of the subject being taught by asking leading questions to get the class to think about and discuss the main points.

This method of instruction is more interesting than a lecture and is ideal for subjects such as current events, topics that require practical exercises (such as First Aid and Map Reading), and topics where a majority of the class is having difficulty learning.

Experienced teachers recommend using a conference when conducting reviews because it enables them to ensure that the class is comfortable with the text material.

Demonstration

Demonstration is a method of instruction that requires class participation. Use this method to show the class how to do a task and to have them practice performing the task. This method holds the students' interest because they are actively involved in the learning process.

Advance planning and preparation are especially important for demonstrations to ensure that everything goes smoothly, and to avoid interruptions or problems that would make the demonstration less realistic.

Practical Exercises

The **practical exercise** is a type of instruction where a learner performs, under controlled conditions, the operation, skill, or procedure being taught. In a practical exercise, class members learn by doing. It is one of the most effective methods for teaching skills. Practical exercises are often used in conjunction with other methods, such as after a lecture or demonstration.

Demonstrations and practical exercises lend themselves to classes such as Leadership Lab, First Aid, Map Reading, and Cadet Challenge.

You will learn more about practical exercises later in this lesson.

Brainstorming

Brainstorming is a problem-solving technique in which instructors give participants a problem and have them bring into the discussion any ideas that come to mind. All ideas are gathered and recorded, without evaluation, before any are discussed. Preferably, the ideas are recorded someplace where all the participants can see them—for example; on a flipchart, whiteboard, or chalkboard.

In some situations, you may limit idea gathering to 5–15 minutes. After gathering the ideas, have the participants discuss them and decide on the best solution or course of action. It is your job, as the instructor, to facilitate this process.

To conduct a successful brainstorming session, you should:

Key Note Term

brainstorming – a teaching method that consists of group problem-solving techniques involving the spontaneous contribution of ideas from all members of the group.

- State the objectives and ground rules of the session up front so that the group members know of the session and what is expected of them

- Encourage input from all group members

- Recognize nonverbal cues that group members want to have input, and respond accordingly

- Keep the session moving and on track

- Avoid judging any ideas offered by the group during the idea-gathering phase

- Facilitate the group by constructively evaluating the various ideas, and in reaching consensus on a solution, idea, or course of action

Case Study

A **case study** is an oral or written account of a real or realistic situation, with sufficient detail to make it possible for the learners to analyze the problems involved and determine possible solutions. There may be many right answers.

Many case study exercises involve group discussions. In this case, you should follow the same rules as described for the discussion/conference. Be prepared to provide relevant and constructive feedback.

Gaming

Gaming consists of activities where participants compete to try to achieve or exceed a certain standard in performing a skill relevant to the learning objectives of the lesson.

Practical Exercise Formats

In the best practical exercises, the tasks that learners perform should be as close as possible to those they will be expected to perform on their assessment or evaluation. The most common types of practical exercises include:

Group Performance/Controlled Exercises

In **group performance**/controlled exercises, learners work together at a fixed rate. Everyone does the same thing at the same time. One caution with this practical exercise type is that learners may imitate the performance without actually understanding it.

Independent Exercises

Learners work alone at their own pace in **independent exercises**. As the instructor, you will circulate around the classroom and supervise, providing assistance and feedback as necessary.

Key Note Term

case study – a teaching method that consists of an oral or written account of a real or realistic situation.

Key Note Term

gaming – a teaching method that consists of activities where participants compete to try and achieve or exceed a certain standard in performing a skill relevant to the learning objectives of the lesson.

Key Note Term

group performance – a controlled practical exercise where learners work together at a fixed rate.

independent exercises – a practical exercise format where learners work alone at their own pace.

Role-playing

In **role-playing** exercises, learners are given different roles to play in a situation, and they apply the concepts being taught while acting out realistic behavior. This type of exercise is especially useful for training interpersonal skills, such as leadership or counseling, or interactive skills in a realistic, but controlled situation.

> **Note**
>
> Role-playing can also be classified as a method of instruction.

Coach-pupil Exercises

In **coach-pupil exercises**, learners work in pairs or small groups, alternately performing as instructor and student. Coach-pupil exercises are extremely useful when time is short or when there are too few instructors.

Team Practical Exercises

In **team practical exercises**, learners work together as a team to perform the desired tasks. This method integrates basic skills into team skills.

Reviews and Rehearsals

As part of your preparation for delivering instruction, you should rehearse prior to attempting to deliver the instruction. Even if you have delivered the instruction many times, rehearsing will help you get into the proper mindset and iron out any problems that you may have had in the past.

Reviews

If you have revised or adapted your materials, review them one last time to ensure you are comfortable with their content, format, and flow. It is also a good idea to look over your references and training aids again.

Rehearse

To help you rehearse, enlist family or friends to serve as an audience and to play the role of students. If possible, practice with all the equipment and training aids you will use in the classroom.

At the conclusion of your instruction, ask your audience to help you evaluate your performance to make sure that you iron out all trouble spots and are conducting the instruction at the proper pace.

Conclusion

Teaching is more than just getting up in front of an audience and talking. You need to develop learning objectives and create a lesson plan identifying the best method for the presentation. Then, you need to review the material and rehearse so you become comfortable delivering the instruction.

If you are asked to instruct others, creating a lesson plan, selecting the most appropriate lesson method, and rehearsing your presentation will increase your confidence level and allow you to conduct a well-received lesson.

Lesson Review

1. Choose one type of teaching method and explain it.

2. Why would one type of teaching method work better than others for different topics and settings?

3. List the most common types of practical exercises.

4. What methods would you choose to review and rehearse before delivering instructions?

Chapter 12

Lesson Review

Lesson 4

Using Variety in Your Lesson Plan

Key Terms

cooperative learning
strategy
team-building exercise

What You Will Learn to Do

- Incorporate a variety of strategies into a lesson plan

Linked Core Abilities

- Communicate using verbal, non-verbal, visual, and written techniques
- Apply critical thinking techniques

Skills and Knowledge You Will Gain along the Way

- Assess the benefits of using cooperative learning strategies in the classroom.
- Select cooperative learning strategies that encourage team-building
- Select cooperative learning strategies that require students to respond to questions posed in the lesson
- Select cooperative learning strategies that help learners gather, share, and learn a great deal of material in a short amount of time
- Explain how incorporating a variety of learning styles and multiple intelligences benefits learners in a classroom
- Define key words contained in this lesson

Chapter 12

Introduction

In the lesson, "Delivering Instruction," you learned a variety of teaching methods, some involving individual effort, and others encompassing group work.

In this lesson you learn how to structure group exercises into a cooperative learning experience for the class.

Cooperative Learning Strategy

A **cooperative learning strategy** is one in which a team of students work with and depend upon each other to accomplish a common goal. Each team member is responsible for:

- **Achieving an individual goal**
- **Instructing the other team members**
- **Receiving information from the other members**
- **Helping their teammates achieve their individual goals**
- **Reaching the group goal**

The team members work both independently and as a group to gather, disseminate, discuss, and incorporate information into a single cohesive element.

A cooperative learning strategy is best used when the learning goals are important, both mastery and retention are important, and the task is complex or conceptual.

As you progress through this lesson, you learn some strategies that can help build good teamwork, strategies that can help students respond to and discuss questions raised in the lesson, strategies that can help students learn the material quickly, and some benefits of cooperative learning.

Team Building Strategies

Teams are composed of a group of individuals associated together in work or activity. Because you are going to form teams when using a cooperative learning strategy, it only makes sense to try and have the best teams possible. Table 12.4.1 shows **team-building exercises** that you can employ to help you foster good team spirit.

> **Key Note Term**
>
> **cooperative learning** – a teaching strategy in which teams of students work with and depend upon each other to accomplish a common goal.

> **Key Note Term**
>
> **team-building exercise** – strategies that can be employed to help foster team dynamics. Examples include team color, name, and logo.

Table 12.4.1: Team-building Exercises

Team Cheer	The team creates a cheer to be used when the group has accomplished a task and is celebrating.
Team Color	The team chooses a color that represents the personality of the group members.
Team Excellence Symbol	The team decides on a physical symbol formed by the group that indicates they have finished an assigned task and that they fulfilled the requirements of the task.
Team Food	The team selects a food (candy, fruit, gum, and so on) that the whole group enjoys and can be used as part of their celebrations.
Team Logo	The team designs a logo that visually represents the group.
Team Name	The group decides on an appropriate name for the team.
Team Song	The team creates a song or selects a song that reflects the group's personality.

Question Strategies

In a standard classroom, the teacher asks questions from time to time and calls on one or more students to answer the question. When a student wants to ask a question, he or she will raise a hand and wait for teacher recognition before speaking.

Group dynamics make the standard question and answer format difficult to use. Table 12.4.2 shows a series of **strategies** that you may employ in a cooperative learning situation to facilitate question response and discussion in a group setting.

Key Note Term

strategy–the art of carefully devising or employing a plan of action or method designed to achieve a goal.

Table 12.4.2: Cooperative Learning Strategies

Heads Together	Pairs of students get together to answer a question, solve a problem, review an assignment, react to a video, generate a discussion, and so on.
Numbered Heads Together	The team members count off (such as one, two, three, four), discuss a problem together, reach some conclusion, then randomly team members answer a question when the teacher calls their number.
Partner Interviews (PI)	Partners take turns interviewing each other to determine their level of understanding of a concept.
Round-Robin	Each team member takes a turn adding information or sharing an idea; each class member shares an insight or new learning; each team member contributes to the creation of a writing project; and so on.
Round-Robin Brainstorm	Team members take turns adding to a group brainstorm.
Squared-Shared-Partner-Interviews	Pairs join with another pair to form a square and share what they gathered from their previous interviews.
Think-Pair-Share (TPS)	Individually, students think about a question, pair with another student to discuss their thoughts, and then share their thoughts with a larger group or with the class.
Team Brainstorm	Team members randomly and rapidly contribute many ideas.

Gather, Share, and Learn Strategies

Despite the good intentions of teachers, events can occur that prohibit them from adhering to their lesson plans (special school assemblies, sickness, inclement weather, and so on). Table 12.4.3 shows several strategies that you may use when you are called upon to teach that will enable the groups to gather, share, and learn their lesson material in a relatively short period of time.

Table 12.4.3: Group Strategies

Carousel	Teams work together to respond to different problems by moving from station to station or by sending their problem around the groups so other groups can contribute to the solution by responding on the chart or paper they receive.
Conversation Circles	Two circles are formed with one circle inside the other. One student from each circle faces another student. In these pairs, students discuss questions posed by the teacher. Circles rotate two to four times in opposite directions so students discuss questions with new partners.
Jigsaw	Material like a chapter in a book, different web sites, several articles, and so on, is segmented and each team member is assigned a segment to study and/or review. Team members return to share their segment with the rest of the group.
Jigsaw and Expert Groups	Each team member is assigned a segment of information. Each member studies the assigned section independently. Members then find others from different groups who studied the same material. Together they review what they learned and reinforce the learning, clarify any misunderstandings, and fill in gaps. They become experts. They return to their original group and share their expertise.
Jigsaw with Expert Groups	Each team member is assigned a segment of information. Each member finds all the others from other groups that share the same assignment. Together, they study the same segment of information and become experts on that information. They return to their original group and share their expertise.
Team Graphic Organizer	Together, a team prepares a single graphic organizer of information.
Team Product or Project	Teams produce a product or engage in a project as a culminating activity.
Team Performance	Teams prepare a performance or presentation based on a synthesis of what they learned.

Benefits of Cooperative Learning

There are benefits for using a **cooperative learning** strategy in the classroom. One of the most important goals in education is to promote constructive relationships and positive attitudes among the student body. The group dynamics of cooperative learning require a large amount of social interaction. Students share ideas and feelings. Team members get to know one another and develop a better understanding of other individuals. The students learn to trust, depend upon, and respect one another as they strive to achieve a common goal. Teammates are appreciated for what they can do and are not simply rejected for what they cannot do.

Cooperative learning groups tend to be more creative than individual students or non-cooperative learning groups because the group dynamics encourage and require all team members to actively participate. More ideas are generated, the quality of ideas is increased, and there is more originality in creative problem solving activities.

Conclusion

Cooperative learning is based on the belief that all people are good at something, have the ability to help others, and can benefit from others' help. This cooperation among all students promotes an exciting and far-reaching way of including differently- enabled students.

By creating a classroom that is cooperative and inclusive, students' acceptance and success in the general education environment will be greatly enhanced. All students and all teachers have much to gain by structuring the classroom and school environment so that it provides generous support for learning, connecting, and caring.

Lesson Review

1. **Describe how cooperative learning is beneficial to the student.**
2. **List the seven team-building strategies covered in this lesson.**
3. **Choose one question strategy and explain how you'd use this in a classroom,**
4. **Choose one gather, share, and learn strategy and explain how you'd use this in a classroom.**

Chapter 12

Lesson Review

Thinking Maps® and Graphic Organizers

Chapter 12

Key Terms

analogy
defining in context
describing
cause and effect reasoning
classifying
comparing and contrasting
part-whole relationship
sequencing
thinking process

What You Will Learn to Do

- Use Thinking Maps® and graphic organizers as tools for teaching others

Linked Core Abilities

- Communicate using verbal, non-verbal, visual, and written techniques

Skills and Knowledge You Will Gain along the Way

- Identify the factors associated with brain-based learning
- Describe the benefits of graphic organizers to the learner
- Compare types of visual tools
- Match thinking processes in learning to Thinking Maps®
- Define key words contained in this lesson

Introduction

Visual tools are excellent tools for learning the structure of thinking skills. Teachers have been using visuals for years to help students make abstract concepts more concrete. These visuals provide a powerful picture of information and allow the mind to "see" patterns and relationships. Some tools are perfect for simple brainstorming; others are task-specific, organizing content. Tools such as Thinking Maps® relate directly to a thinking skill or process.

Graphic organizers and Thinking Maps® are both based on the brain and educational research that supports the use of visuals in a classroom. According to Eric Jensen in his book *Teaching with the Brain in Mind,* 90 percent of all information that comes to the brain is visual. Robert Marzano's *Classroom Instruction That Works* cites research that proves that using visuals in a classroom improves student achievement.

Each kind of visual tool can encourage student-centered and cooperative learning. The JROTC curriculum uses both graphic organizers and Thinking Maps within its lesson plans. In this lesson, you examine the various types of visual tools and use them as you continue to improve your teaching skills.

Types of Visual Tools

There are three basic types of visual tools for learning and enhancing the **thinking process**. These can be defined as brainstorm "webs," task-specific graphic organizers, and Thinking Maps®.

Brainstorm Webs

Brainstorm webs are visual tools used for personal knowledge, and include mind mapping and webbing.

A mind map is a form of brainstorming using a free-flowing documentation process where lines connect concepts to each other. The core subject is in the center; the main spokes are like sub parts of chapters. Related ideas can be color coded, circled, or attached by lines. Pictures and words can both be used. For example, you could use this tool to discuss what it will take for a cadet to successfully earn a high school diploma.

Key Note Term

thinking process – the organized way in which thinking occurs.

Step	Action	Graphic
1	Set up chart paper on easel and get the markers. If possible place the paper in a horizontal position.	
2	Draw the central concept on the paper. Ask the cadets to define what the concept is—for example, graduate from high school.	
3	The cadets will brainstorm what it takes to graduate and draw pictures or images to show these items—for example, money, books, studying, and ideas are some of the information they could provide.	
4	Link the thoughts to show relationships of ideas—for example, books are needed before you can study and get your degree. Ideas as well as money are independent ideas that support receiving a degree.	

The concept web uses text to link main concepts and sub-concepts or even sub-sub- concepts. The center circle is the main concept or idea. The smaller circles connecting to the main concept represent the sub-concepts; connected to these sub-concepts are sub-sub-concepts. For example, the center circle could be citizenship. The smaller connected circles are sub-concepts related to citizenship.

These smaller circles can also be explored for additional supporting concepts. An illustration might be the sub concept of voting as a critical part of citizenship. Most cadets can't vote yet, but they could continue to explore how they might encourage voting or how they might get involved with the voting process.

Step	Action	Graphic
1	Set up chart paper on easel and get the markers. If possible place the paper in a horizontal position.	
2	Draw a circle in the center of the paper with a diameter sufficient to hold the main idea and write the main idea in the circle.	Citizenship
3	Draw a connected sub-concept containing a concept related to the main concept.	Vote — Citizenship
4	Draw a ray out from the sub-concept and place an element of voting on the ray. Add additional rays as needed.	Age, Vote, Citizenship
5	Add additional sub-concepts with rays as needed to cover all the elements.	Age, Vote, Citizenship, Tax, Fight

When using these tools in a teaching environment, you can ask the students to use any of these types of "webs" to brainstorm a topic of their choice. They are very effectively used during the Inquire phase of our lesson plans. Students can complete this activity alone, in pairs, or as a group. An example of how they can be used is to have students complete a web individually. Then pair up and exchange their notes. Each student should read his or her partner's web ideas and try to summarize the concept being brainstormed without any help from the cadet who created the visual. Paired students should then discuss their summaries.

Task-specific Graphic Organizers

Task-specific graphic organizers are used for isolated tasks, and are found in different textbooks. They are used to represent life cycles, timelines, and other content-specific data. One example is the Fishbone Diagram.

This structure helps cadets think of important components of a problem to solve, an issue to explore, or a project to plan. The head of the fish represents a problem, issue, or project. "Ribs" of the fish represent component parts of the problem and the related elements of each part. For example, cadets could explore how to prepare for an upcoming orienteering competition. Each rib represents the critical elements of preparation. Attached to each rib are the processes or activities that will assist in accomplishing each key element.

An example of how to use task-specific graphic organizers in a teaching environment is to have students work in pairs to survey their textbooks or other resources to look for content that could be represented by graphic organizers and visuals, such as the steps to determine direction of travel, or the timeline for how the framers created the constitution. Then have students choose and draw graphic organizers to represent their thinking about the subject or topic.

Thinking Maps®

Thinking Maps® give students and teachers a common visual language for learning that can be used with all subject matter and across all LET levels in classrooms and whole schools. The purpose for using them is to transfer thinking processes, integrate learning, and assess progress. Thinking Maps® consist of eight graphics or "Maps." Each one is tied directly to a specific thinking process. Look at the key word definitions for each map and notice how they are used to organize your thinking.

> **Note**
>
> The introductory "Thinking Maps®" lesson contains pictures of each type of map discussed here.

Thinking Maps® are most effective when they are used together to develop a learning objective, concept, or performance task. An example of how multiple maps can be used to develop an understanding of heat injuries can be seen in Figure 12.5.1.

Step	Action	Graphic
1	Set up chart paper on easel and get the markers. If possible place the paper in a horizontal position.	
2	Draw a square about the size of a CD-ROM case. This will be the head.	
3	Draw a horizontal line from the left side of the head to the left side of the paper. This is the backbone.	
4	Draw ribs out from the backbone above and below the backbone. Make sure they correspond and touch each other at the intersection. Add rays as needed.	
5	Instruct the cadets to write their responses for one point of view on the bottom set of bones and the other point of view on the top. EXAMPLE: On the bottom write: Problems On the top write: Materials and Transportation	Map, Compass, Markers — Materials; Car, Truck, Bus, Train — Transportation; Water, Magnetism — Problems; Access, Amount, Cost, Drivers — Problems

Figure 12.5.1: Using multiple maps.

Circle Map: *Brainstorm what you know about signs and symptoms of heat injury.*

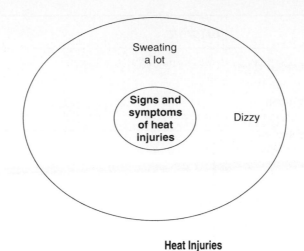

Tree Map: *Classify the types of heat injuries.*

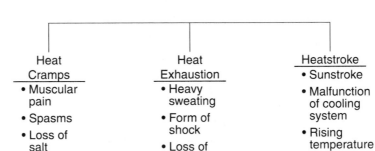

Flow Map: *Sequence the steps to treat heatstroke.*

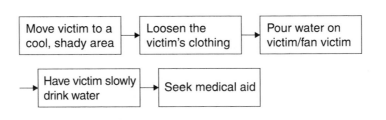

Bridge Map: *Show the relationship between each type of heat injury.*

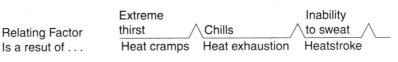

*Extreme thirst is a result of heat cramps, just as chills is a result of heat exhaustion, just as the inability to sweat is a result of heatstroke.

Multi-Flow Map: *Show the causes and effects of heat injuries.*

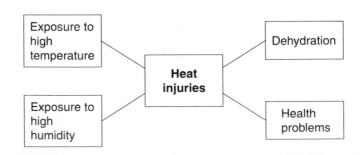

Putting them all together

As closure for the three preceding activities, ask cadets to draw some conclusions about the effectiveness of these three different types of visual tools.

Comparing Thinking Maps® to Other Graphic Organizers

Graphic organizers and webs are commonly used strategies that help organize and process a great deal of information. They can help make relationships and connections visible or concrete. Thinking Maps® combine the flexibility of brainstorm webs and the structure of task-specific graphic organizers with a clearly defined, common thinking process language. Graphic organizers and webs help people graphically organize information. Thinking Maps® help people think about their information and construct knowledge.

The most important difference between Thinking Maps® and graphic organizers is that each Thinking Map® is based on a fundamental thinking skill.

This thinking skills foundation supports three intellectual outcomes:

- **Students learn clearly stated definitions for eight fundamental thinking skills.**
- **Students are applying multiple thinking skills (as Maps) to complex, multistep problems.**
- **Students are empowered to use these visual tools for transferring thinking skills across disciplines.**

The Double Bubble Map in Figure 12.5.2 compares the similarities and differences between graphic organizers and webs and Thinking Maps®.

Figure 12.5.2: Similarities and differences.
Copyright © 2004 by Thinking Maps, Inc.

Double Bubble: *Explain the similarities and differences of heat exhaustion and heat stroke.*

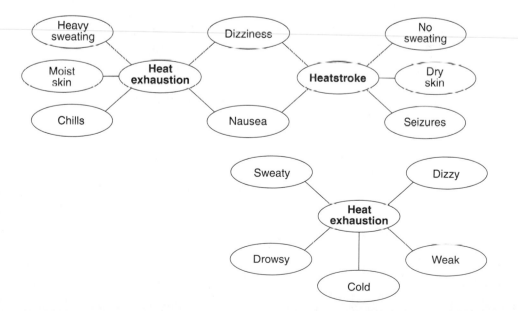

Bubble Map: *Describe how a person would feel if they had heat exhaustion.*

Which Visual Tool Do I Choose?

As you are reading content or listening to someone speak, your brain is processing the information by figuring out what to do with it. When that happens, the next step is to visualize a graphic organizer, web or a Thinking Map® that can help you understand and remember the information. If, for example, the information you receive is asking you to define something, you may choose to use a mind map, a concept map, or a Circle Map as illustrated earlier in this lesson. If you are being asked to compare and contrast something, you may choose to use a Venn Diagram or a Double Bubble Map. Graphic organizers, webs, and Thinking Maps® have proven to be highly successful for the learner. When considering which visual tool to use, remember that Thinking Maps® are consistently used for a specific thinking process while the other tools are less defined and therefore are not always used in the same way for the same purpose.

Look at the example in Figure 12.5.3. Discuss with a partner or group which visual tool you feel is most beneficial and effective for learning. What are the advantages and disadvantages of each?

Figure 12.5.3: Contrasting and comparing visual tools.
Copyright © 2004 by Thinking Maps, Inc.

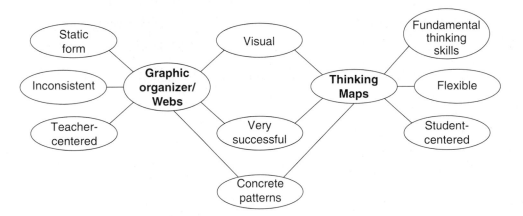

Now practice picking a visual tool for learning. Think about a specific task you might do in JROTC. Choose a graphic organizer and a Thinking Map® to represent the same tasks. Share why the visual tools were chosen and which will help you retain the information the most.

Use the Double Bubble Map to help you remember the similarities and differences between Thinking Maps® and other graphic organizers.

Conclusion

Overall, Thinking Maps® and graphic organizers allow you to visually organize concepts, ideas, data, thoughts, and feelings. Choosing the appropriate Map or graphic organizer depends on the type of elements that need organizing and analyzing. After the organization process is complete, understanding complex concepts, decision-making, and problem-solving becomes easier.

Lesson Review

1. Name and describe the three types of visual tools.
2. What are the similarities and differences between Thinking Maps® and other graphic organizers?
3. What are the advantages and/or disadvantages of using Thinking Maps®?
4. What are the advantages and/or disadvantages of using graphic organizers and webs?

Chapter 12

Lesson Review

Lesson 6

Using Feedback in the Classroom

Key Terms

acceptable
clarify
comprehensive
constructive
conviction
criteria
flexible
jargon
modify
objectivity
preconceived
rapport
reinforce

What You Will Learn to Do

- Use feedback to enhance learning in the classroom

Linked Core Abilities

- Communicate using verbal, non-verbal, visual, and written techniques

Skills and Knowledge You Will Gain along the Way

- Describe the purpose of feedback in the classroom
- Explain four ways that feedback can be effective
- Identify the five characteristics or conditions of effective feedback
- Identify the basic ground rules and tips for giving effective feedback
- Define key words contained in this lesson

Chapter 12

Introduction

In traditional courses individualized comments from instructors to their students are often limited to grades on papers, quizzes, exams, and the final grade; however, comments of this sort come well after instructors have evaluated learners on their course work. Such after-the-fact feedback often contributes little to learning because it is too late for learners to take corrective action. On the other hand, the most important task you have as an instructor may be to provide information that learners can use to improve themselves during the course. Such feedback guides learners while they can still take corrective action.

This lesson examines how you can give **objective**, **acceptable**, **constructive**, **flexible**, and **comprehensive** feedback.

Definitions and Applications

In general, feedback is any information about the results of a process. When you use a computer, for instance, you feed in the information and get back feedback. In the social sciences, feedback is the information that returns to the source of the process so as to **reinforce** or **modify** it. For example, if a coach finds that the football team is weak in defense tactics, the coach schedules the team for more tackling practice. In psychological **jargon**, feedback is called the "knowledge of results."

In the classroom, feedback can be defined as information that learners receive from their instructor about their performance, information that may cause them to take self-corrective action and guide them in attaining the goals of the course more effectively.

Learners can receive feedback from at least five sources: themselves, the learning task, fellow cadets/students, the instructor, and from the school/cadet battalion.

Feedback is generally given for informational and/or motivational purposes. Informational feedback is generally responsible for correcting the errors that the learner commits and should always be motivating. Motivational feedback motivates the learner to try harder but does not always provide information. A pat on the back or a word of encouragement may motivate a learner, but will not necessarily point out the errors in the learner's performance.

Giving Feedback to Learners

The purpose of giving feedback in the classroom is to improve learner performance. In its most effective form, it provides constructive advice, direction, and guidance to learners in their effort to raise their performance levels. Learners must understand the purpose and role of feedback in the learning process; otherwise, they may reject it and make little or no effort to improve.

Key Note Term

objective – dealing with facts or conditions as perceived without distortion by personal feelings, prejudices, or interpretations.

acceptable – capable or worthy of being accepted, adequate, satisfactory.

constructive – promoting improvement or development.

flexible – ready to adapt to new, different, or changing requirements.

comprehensive – covering completely or broadly.

Key Note Term

reinforce – to strengthen by additional assistance, material, or support.

modify – to make basic or fundamental changes to give a new orientation to or to serve a new end.

jargon – technical terminology or language created for a particular profession, such as computer science, that may seem strange or outlandish to outsiders who do not understand it.

Feedback can also be used as a device to reinforce learning. Although all feedback cannot be used in this manner, the instructor should take every opportunity to use feedback as a means of **clarifying**, emphasizing, or reinforcing instruction.

Characteristics (or Conditions) of Effective Feedback

Effective feedback stresses both learner strengths as well as suggestions for improvement. The most significant characteristics, or conditions, of effective feedback are objectivity, acceptability, constructiveness, flexibility, and comprehensiveness. Each of these characteristics is briefly explained in the following sections.

Objectivity

Effective feedback focuses on the learner and the learner's performance; it should not reflect the instructor's personal opinions, likes, and biases. For example, if the learner makes a speech and expresses views that conflict with the your beliefs, you should give feedback on the merits of the speech, not on the basis of the agreement or disagreement with the learner's views. To be objective, feedback must be honest; it must be based on factual performance—not performance as it could have been or as you and the learner wish it had been.

Acceptability

Learners usually accept feedback when you give it with **conviction** and sincerity. Usually, you have the opportunity to establish **rapport** and mutual respect with learners before the need for giving feedback arises. If there is no such opportunity, your manner, attitude, and knowledge of the subject must serve instead.

Constructiveness

You must be straightforward and honest; you must also respect the learner's personal feelings. Feedback, then, is pointless unless the learner profits from it. Praise just for the sake of praise has no value; however, unless the only goal is to motivate or improve self-concept.

Effective feedback reflects your consideration of the learner's need for self-esteem, recognition, confidence, and the approval of others. Ridicule, anger, or fun at the expense of the learner have no place in constructive feedback.

Flexibility

You should always remain flexible in giving feedback by avoiding mechanical, predetermined techniques and **preconceived** opinions regarding content, subject matter, and learner capability. Instead, you should consider:

Key Note Term

clarify – to make understandable.

Key Note Term

conviction – a strong persuasion or belief.

rapport – a relationship, especially one of mutual trust.

Key Note Term

preconceived – to form (as an opinion) prior to actual knowledge or experience.

- **The actual content of the learner's effort**
- **What actually happens during an activity**
- **The observed factors that affect performance**

Comprehensiveness

Comprehensive feedback need not be extremely long nor must it treat every detail of the learner's performance. As an instructor, you must decide whether you can achieve the best results by discussing a few major points or a number of minor points. You should base your feedback either on what areas need improvement or on what areas you can reasonably expect the learner to improve.

Feedback includes both strengths and weaknesses. Only you can determine a proper balance between the two. It is a disservice to learners to dwell on the excellence of their performance and neglect areas that need improving (or vise versa).

Ground Rules and Tips for Giving Feedback

There are some basic ground rules for giving feedback so it is constructive and helpful to the learner. These rules include:

- **Establish and maintain rapport with learners.**
- **Cover the major strengths and weaknesses. Try to be specific; give examples if possible.**
- **Avoid trying to discuss everything. A few well-made points may be more beneficial than numerous, but inadequately developed points.**
- **Try to avoid comments with "never" or "always"; most rules have exceptions. Your feedback may be incorrect or inappropriate for certain situations.**
- **Do not criticize something that cannot be corrected.**
- **Do not criticize when you cannot suggest an improvement.**
- **Avoid being maneuvered into the unpleasant position of defending feedback. If the feedback is honest, objective, constructive, and supported, no defense should be necessary.**
- **If part of the feedback is written, it should be consistent with the oral feedback.**

To ensure the learner takes your feedback in the most constructive manner possible and use it in a positive way, the following tips can be helpful.

- **Reinforce correct performance by letting learners know what they are doing well. Your encouragement and support will mean a great deal to your learners.**
- **Make sure to base your feedback on the evaluation criteria.**
- **When you see someone doing something differently than you would ordinarily do it, consider whether it matters. Ask yourself questions such as:**

> **Key Note Term**
>
> **criteria** – a standard on which a judgment or decision is based.

- Will it work the way he/she, they are doing it?
- Is this a better way?
- Will it cause problems for them later?
- Is it safe?

- Allow for individual variations. Consider the learner's openness to suggestions before recommending changes that are not based on the criteria.
- Identify incorrect performance as early as possible. Give feedback as soon as you see the incorrect performance.
- Try to provide feedback in the most constructive way possible. Help learners understand how to do a task correctly—do not just tell them what they are doing wrong.
- Be aware of the learners' sensitivity to correction, especially in front of other people (generally avoided whenever possible). Keep your voice down when providing individual feedback. Avoid the temptation to point out one person's mistake to the whole group as an example.
- Give feedback less often as learners progress.

Conclusion

It is important to realize that feedback need not always be negative or destructive. In fact, positive feedback is almost always seen as warmer and more sincere than negative feedback given in identical ways.

As a potential instructor, coach, and counselor in JROTC, you must be able to give effective, positive feedback. By improving the way that you give feedback, you are improving the future performances of your teammates and classmates.

Lesson Review

1. Why feedback is generally given?
2. What are the characteristics of feedback covered in this lesson?
3. Choose one tip for giving feedback and discuss it.
4. Define the term "criteria."

Chapter 12

Lesson Review

Mandatory Core
Service Learning

Chapter 8

Making a Difference with Service Learning

Lesson 1

Orientation to Service Learning

Key Terms

community service
debriefer
facilitator
orientation
recorder
reflection
reporter
service learning
timekeeper

What You Will Learn to Do

- Identify the components of service learning

Linked Core Abilities

- Apply critical thinking techniques

Skills and Knowledge You Will Gain Along the Way

- Compare the types of service opportunities within your community
- Identify the benefits of serving others within a community
- Associate the roles and responsibilities of service learning teams
- Define key words contained in this lesson

Chapter 8

Introduction

You have probably noticed that people who seem to find the most satisfaction in life are those actively engaged in doing something to make the world a better place for everyone. They seem happy because they are making a difference. Have you ever helped a friend through a difficult time or done something similar to stopping to help change a flat tire or take food to a sick neighbor? Then you know why people who help others appear to be more genuinely content with their lives.

Unfortunately, although you know you will feel good, it is probably not easy for you to get started. You are not alone. Many people find it awkward to reach out. However, after you take those initial steps and begin making a difference, the difficulties disappear. Feelings of accomplishment and generosity of spirit make the effort and time you spent worthwhile.

So how do you get started in service? First, look around you. There are problems and people in need everywhere. You do not have to look very far to find hunger, illiteracy, pollution, illness, poverty, neglect, and loneliness. Decide on an urgent need or one that you find most compelling. What matters most is that you make a commitment to address the need in a positive way.

After you have chosen a need, select a project that will help you accomplish your goal of making a difference. President John F. Kennedy reminded everyone to, "Ask not what your country can do for you; ask what you can do for your country." Planning and carrying out the **service learning** project will help you selflessly "do" for your neighbor, your community, your state, your country, and the world.

The author Aldous Huxley said, "Experience is not what happens to you; it's what you do with what happens to you." Service learning takes that belief to heart. It is not enough to take positive actions, you must learn from your actions. For example, starting a paper recycling program is a worthy project; it can become more meaningful when you learn more about why it is important, reflect on your experiences, identify what you learned, analyze how you've changed, and decide other ways you can recycle and help others commit to recycling.

Service learning experiences can become the starting point for self-awareness, self-improvement, and self-fulfillment. In the process of making a difference for others, you make a difference in yourself.

What Is Service Learning?

Service learning is an active and experiential learning strategy where students have a direct impact on an identified need that interests and motivates them. It requires sequential lessons that are organized so **orientation** and training come before the meaningful service activity and structured reflection follows the activity.

Key Note Term

service learning – an environment where one can learn and develop by actively participating in organized service experiences within one's own community.

Key Note Term

orientation – the act or process of orienting or being oriented, such as being oriented on the first day of college.

> Orientation and Training
>
> + Meaningful Service
>
> + Structured Reflection
>
> SERVICE LEARNING

Structured Teamwork

Service learning requires active participation in structured teamwork. Working within small teams and solving problems together will help you become active participants. Each member is assigned a team role, including:

- **Facilitator** (The facilitator leads team discussions to identify needs and prepare service learning activities.)
- **Recorder** (The recorder takes notes for the team and organizes information.)
- **Reporter** (The reporter represents the team voice and reports team findings.)
- **Timekeeper** (The timekeeper keeps track of time and plans the schedule.)
- **Debriefer** (The debriefer encourages team members and leads discussion after presentation.)

Cadet teams should determine, plan, and execute service-learning activities with the aid of their instructor.

Orientation and Training

Orientation and training activities are necessary to prepare you and other participants for the service experience. Integrating what you are learning in class with the service activity is a key goal of service learning. This step requires in-class lessons, followed by selecting a service project that relates to the curriculum and meets academic standards.

You should be familiar enough with the material to conduct the service project you have selected. Part of the planning process will require you to determine what you need to know before the activity and to train yourself accordingly.

If possible, speak with representatives or others involved with the service you have selected to see what to expect. Orient yourself with the service goals, those you will be helping, other organizations or people that you may need to contact, and so on. In other words, learn what you need to know before starting the service experience and plan for all potential circumstances.

Key Note Terms

facilitator – one who facilitates; one who leads team discussion.

recorder – one who take notes for the team and organizes information.

reporter – one who represents the team voice and reports team findings.

timekeeper – one who keeps track of time and plans the schedule.

debriefer – one who encourages team members and leads discussions after presentation and team discussion.

Meaningful Service

It is your responsibility to initiate and plan service activities to correspond to the lesson material. Although there should be at least 15 cadets per service experience, you can either work in committees on one project or small teams on separate projects. For example, you may want to divide the project components among three teams of five cadets each. Learning should be an active and social experience that is meaningful to you and those involved. Within your teams, choose a service activity that:

- **Addresses a real and important need another group is not addressing**
- **Is interesting and challenging**
- **Connects you to others within the community or world**
- **Challenges you to develop new skills**
- **Requires little or no money**
- **Is achievable within the time available**
- **Has a positive effect on others**

Structured Reflection

Reflection, or taking time to observe, analyze, and integrate actions with learning, is an important part of the learning process. A strong reflection helps you develop skills and extend learning from the service experience. You may use many types of reflection: learning logs and essays; team and class discussions; performances; graphic organizers; and public presentations. Using learning logs throughout the experience to record thoughts, feelings, knowledge and processes will help you organize what you have learned.

Within your teams, share what you have learned by discussing your answers to open-ended questions before, during, and after each service experience. Reflection questions should encourage observation, analysis and integration.

Community Service Versus Service Learning

Community service in many states is dispensed by a judge or court system as mandatory work for infractions of the law. Some students and members of the community view this type of service as punishment. What students learn is that they don't ever want to be forced to do "service" again. Today, many high schools include community service hours as a graduation requirement and though intentions are good, sometimes the emphasis is on quantity of hours, not quality of the project.

Service learning, on the other hand, is a step up from community service; it brings academics to life and is driven by student involvement. You should identify essential needs in your school or community, and then decide on your own projects. In addition, you should plan and carry out your own projects and take responsibility for your own learning. Reflecting on the experience will reveal the importance of your service work and the impact you are making on yourself and others.

Key Note Term

reflection – a thought, idea, or opinion formed or a remark made as a result of mediation; consideration of some subject matter, idea, or purpose.

Key Note Term

community service – any form of service provided for the community or common good.

Why Use Service Learning?

Service learning is rapidly growing in popularity around the country. Students who are able to learn about the world around them and work to improve it as part of their education reap many benefits. Such students:

- **Learn more**
- **Earn better grades**
- **Come to school more often**
- **Demonstrate better behavior**
- **Become more civic minded**
- **Gain a first-hand appreciation and understanding of people from other cultures, races, and generations**
- **See the connections between school and "real life"**
- **Feel better about themselves**
- **Learn skills they can use after leaving school**

Service learning provides a safe environment where you can learn, make mistakes, have successes, and develop by actively participating in organized service experiences within your community. For example, such experiences might include:

- **Meeting actual community needs by providing meaningful service**
- **Coordinating in partnership with the school and community**
- **Integrating these service opportunities into an academic curriculum, thereby enhancing what your school teaches, extending your learning beyond the classroom, and offering unique learning experiences**
- **Providing you with opportunities to use previously and newly acquired academic skills and knowledge in real-life situations in your own community**
- **Providing structured time for you to think, talk, and write about what you did and saw during your actual service activity**
- **Helping you to develop a sense of caring for others**

Providing service can be a powerful tool in the development of attitudes and behavior. It can transform young adults from passive recipients into active providers, and in so doing, redefine the perception of their involvement in the community from a cause of problems to a source of solutions.

Important skills you will need to work successfully to accomplish each service learning activity are similar to those identified in the Secretary's Commission on Achieving Necessary Skills (SCANS) report. There are several important skills and qualities identified in the SCANS to ensure students are prepared for the workforce. The following are just a few of those skills service learning can help you strengthen.

- Being an effective team member
- Providing resource and time management
- Engaging in frequent and effective communication
- Making decisions
- Organizing and being responsible
- Effectively managing personal problems such as poor writing skills, lack of research skills, or stereotyping

Conclusion

When combined with formal education, service becomes a method of learning or "service learning." Learning is maximized by combining the three main service learning components: orientation and training, meaningful service, and structured reflection.

Service learning is the single learning strategy that can accomplish the most good for the greatest number of people. Studies suggest that service learning reinforces curriculum content and standards, and benefits participants academically, as well as personally and socially. By getting involved to help meet different needs, you have the potential to make a difference to someone specific or to the entire community.

Lesson Review

1. Who do you know that might benefit from your participation in service learning?
2. Define the term "learning logs."
3. Compare and contrast community service and service learning.
4. List five benefits from your participation in service learning.

Chapter 8

Lesson Review

Plan and Train for Your Exploratory Project

Chapter 8

Key Terms

experimental learning
exploratory project
field education
problem-based learning
training

What You Will Learn to Do

- Prepare for a service learning project

Linked Core Abilities

- Build your capacity for life-long learning
- Communicate using verbal, non-verbal, visual, and written techniques
- Do your share as a good citizen in your school, community, country, and the world

Skills and Knowledge You Will Gain Along the Way

- Select an exploratory project
- Identify the steps needed to conduct a service learning experience

- Identify the essential components of a chosen service learning project
- Develop a plan addressing various circumstances and outcomes of the project
- Define key words contained in this lesson

Introduction

Key Note Terms

exploratory project – a teacher-planned introductory project to service learning, intended to provide students with a meaningful experience, expose them to how it feels to serve, and to stimulate their thinking abut possible service learning activities.

experiential learning – gaining practical knowledge, skills, or practice from direct observation of or participation in events or in a particular activity.

problem-based learning – an instructional strategy that promotes active learning where problems form the focus and learning stimulus and problem-solving skills are utilized.

There are several points to consider before undergoing service learning. Planning ahead will prepare you both mentally and physically to undertake the challenge. Before you select a service learning project in class, your instructor should familiarize you with service learning by guiding you in an **exploratory project** within the community. This will help you select a service project and demonstrate the steps to conducting a proper service learning experience.

Exploratory Project Purpose

The exploratory project is an introduction to a service learning activity that utilizes **experiential learning** and **problem-based learning** principles. The purpose of a teacher-planned exploratory project is to provide students with a meaningful experience, expose them to how it feels to serve, and to stimulate their thinking about possible service learning activities.

One of the primary benefits of engaging in an exploratory project is to understand what service learning entails. Service learning is not community service, although many confuse the two. Until you participate in service learning, you will not have a real-life experience to justify the difference.

Exploratory projects help you capture a vision of how to make a difference in the world. After you get involved, you may begin to see the world through different glasses. In addition, as you work to address one need in the community, several other unmet needs will begin to surface. Your vision of the world may change when you begin to see critical needs where you never saw them before.

Suggested introductory projects could include going to a hospital or nursing home to visit residents, distributing food at a food bank, or volunteering at a local Red Cross program.

Service Learning Steps

Before participating in service, familiarize yourself with the following steps to conduct a proper service learning experience:

1. Complete a pre-assessment of skill level using the Personal Skills Map from the JROTC Success Profiler.

2. Determine a school, community, or national need you can fill relating to class curriculum.

3. Brainstorm and select a meaningful service project that meets proposed guidelines.

4. Start a learning log to record new knowledge, thoughts and feelings throughout all phases.

5. Plan and organize details of the service activity and discuss expectations.

6. Participate in a meaningful service activity that meets the service learning guidelines (Form 219-R).

7. Discuss and reflect on what you experienced (observation).

8. Discuss and reflect on what you gained from the experience (analysis).

9. Discuss and reflect on what you can do with the new information (integration).

10. Complete a project summary report and a final group evaluation form to judge teamwork and other activities.

11. Brief the experience to community members, administration, classmates, and so on.

12. Complete a post-assessment using the Personal Skills Map and related analysis to determine a plan of action.

Choosing a Service Activity

After participating in an exploratory project, you should be able to select your own service activity that meets an important need and integrates the curriculum.

It is very important that you participate in selecting a service activity that is meaningful to you and others. Brainstorm service ideas relative to the lesson curriculum and program at hand. Then as a class or team, select the service activity.

Service learning opportunities can use **field education** principles to incorporate scholastic programs with the curriculum. You can integrate programs such as:

- **Lions-Quest Skills for Action®**
- **Groundhog Job Shadow Day®**
- **NEFE High School Financial Planning Program®**
- **You the People®**
- **Chief Justice®**
- **Cadet Ride®**

Key Note Term

field education – performing service and training to enhance understanding with a field of study.

In field education, you perform the service as a part of a **training** program designed primarily to enhance understanding of a field of study while providing substantial emphasis on the service.

Besides integrating curriculum and service, you will learn more about the different types, models, and terms of service in the next lesson, "Project Reflection and Integration."

Planning the Service

After you have chosen an activity, you must plan the essential facets for project completion and prepare or train yourself for what is to come.

This is where service learning begins. Service learning efforts should start with clearly stated goals and development of a plan of action that encourages cadet responsibility. You can achieve those goals through structured preparation and brainstorming such as discussion, writing, reading, observation, and the service itself. Keep the goals consistent with the level of the activity planned and ensure that the goals and plan of action draw upon the skills and knowledge of your team. When corresponding goals to the curriculum, try to determine academic content standards you will address through the service.

Besides determining goals and standards, plans should be comprehensive to ensure adequate preparation for each step or task. Determine a description of the task(s) and answer the questions:

- **Who will be involved?**
- **What is involved and needs to be done?**
- **When will each step take place?**
- **Where will it all take place?**
- **Why will we do it?**
- **How will it work?**

For example, you might decide to visit a local veterans hospital. You could discover the needs of the elderly patients that reside there by discussions with the hospital's administrative personnel or possibly by meeting with the residents themselves. You should also determine where the project fits into the curriculum. Together, you might decide that the patients need to have younger people help them write letters to family members, assist with their wellness and fitness, or plan and lead activities.

If you are aware of children who have a hard time learning to read, you could plan a service activity to a local elementary school. Because teachers rarely have extra time on their hands to spend one-on-one with those children, certain schools may welcome JROTC cadets who could come and spend time reading or listening to the children read. You do not have to limit this service to reading. Consider helping in mathematics or other subjects. Remember to maximize the use of your participating cadets' skills and knowledge. Contact your local Junior Achievement office at http://www.ja.org for more service learning suggestions to help teach elementary students. You can also find service learning project ideas by searching the Internet.

Do not forget to accomplish the administrative details during the preparation phase. Teams often overlook these requirements or assume that someone else will do them. You must obtain permission from school administrators to conduct the service learning activity as a field trip and arrange for transportation, lunch, and parental release/permission slips for participating cadets, and the necessary supplies and equipment to perform the activity. Invite administrators, counselors, community members, and so on to be on your Advisory Board so that they will become more involved with your project.

Training for the Service

Before participating in the service activity, prepare yourself for different circumstances or outcomes. This may involve learning about the subject matter you will be expected to know to complete the tasks you have laid out, or discussing different outcomes and expectations within your teams. Try your best to be prepared for different situations you may encounter. Within teams, or as a class, brainstorm and discuss potential hazards you may encounter, and precautions you should take to make the task run smoothly.

Pretend you are taking a bus to a children's hospital with a group of cadets to tutor sick children who cannot be in school. You may need to train yourselves on particular academic subjects/content, research what grade levels will be represented, and locate the hospital. Also, make sure to pair up and plan a meeting time and place.

Executing the Service

In this phase, there are a few rules to remember. Arrive on time and always be courteous. You are representing your school and you should act accordingly at all times. Also, ensure that you understand the task or goal at hand. If you are not sure, ask an authority. They should be able to point you in the right direction. If you are a team leader, make sure your team members feel completely comfortable with the tasks. Finally, if a situation or problem arises that needs an authority's attention (for example, an accident occurs and someone is hurt), take what actions you can and have someone contact the person in charge.

Being well organized and completely prepared are fundamental for a successful execution phase. For example, if you are going to build a garden such as the one mentioned earlier in this lesson:

Service Learning Success Story

During lessons on Planning and Social Responsibility, cadets in Gastonia, North Carolina, decided to plant a garden at a nursing home. Their pre-planning resulted in a specially designed, waist-high "no stoop garden" so seniors could help maintain the plants and flowers. This is a good example of how the needs of the elderly were taken into consideration when the garden plan was developed.

- Ensure you have the correct tools and supplies to complete the service.
- Know the name or names of the contacts for the particular service you are performing.
- Identify alternate group leaders in case there are absences.
- Assign cadets to work on projects according to their experience and abilities.
- Be thoroughly prepared to complete the task, but be flexible to make changes. Things may not go as you plan them.

Remember, you are there to render a service for your community.

Conclusion

The exploratory project will introduce you to service learning through active participation. From there, you will be ready to choose your own service activity. At that time, remember that good planning is the key to a successful service learning venture. Training may be necessary to complete the task, and learning should be the focus as well as making a difference through service.

You should now be prepared to use the proposed steps and planning procedures to conduct a proper service learning experience.

Lesson Review

1. Define the term "problem-based learning."
2. Why is it important to participate in a service activity that means something to you?
3. What materials might you need if you were visiting children in a hospital?
4. Name three projects in your community you might want to join.
5. What are the steps needed to conduct a service learning experience?

Lesson 3

Project Reflection and Integration

Key Terms

advocacy service
after action review
analysis
direct service
indirect service
integration
observation
placement
project

What You Will Learn to Do

- Evaluate the effectiveness of a service learning project

Linked Core Abilities

- Communicate using verbal, non-verbal, visual, and written techniques
- Apply critical thinking techniques

Skills and Knowledge You Will Gain Along the Way

- Relate the projected goals of a service learning project to the final outcomes
- Identify ways to integrate service learning into the JROTC curriculum
- Outline service learning objectives for the future
- Define key words

Chapter 8

Introduction

Now that you have an idea of what service learning is all about, what comes next? After the exploratory project, you will be able to determine and conduct appropriate service learning activities. Before choosing activities, you should know about the models, terms, and types of service available, and how to integrate service with what you are learning in class.

After you have completed a service activity, you should follow it up with a structured reflection, demonstration of learning, and evaluation of the service learning.

Short-term Versus Long-term Service

You need to understand how to meet others' needs through either short-term or long-term service activities. Short-term service projects include:

- **Restoring a historical monument during history lessons**
- **Raising money at an event for charity during financial planning lessons**
- **Visiting a nursing home while discussing wellness and fitness issues**

Long-term service projects include:

- **Adopting a local waterway while studying environmental issues**
- **Setting up an advocacy campaign to raise financial resources for shelters during financial planning lessons**
- **Organizing an after-school tutoring program during lessons on teaching skills**

Models of Service

Service can be done anywhere to reinforce what you are learning in class; you do not even have to leave the school grounds. The two models of service include **projects** and **placements**.

Project Model

Service learning projects are initiated and planned by cadets with instructor guidance. Tutoring elementary children in subjects you are currently studying or starting a recycling program based on information from your geography lessons are examples of service projects.

Key Note Terms

projects – a task or problem engaged in usually by a group of students to supplement and apply classroom studies; service learning projects are initiated and planned by cadets with instructor guidance.

placement – service learning activities carried out beyond the classroom in a pre-existing, structured situation.

Placement Model

Service learning placements are activities carried out beyond the classroom in a preexisting, structured situation. The placement organization typically assigns responsibilities to students individually. Examples include: teaching lessons for Junior Achievement, or volunteering for Special Olympics during fitness lessons.

Three Types of Service

The three types of service are **direct**, **indirect**, and **advocacy**. These service types are described in the following sections.

Direct Service

Direct service involves face-to-face contact with those being served in either project or placement models of service learning. Examples of direct service include working in a soup kitchen or working with disadvantaged children while you are studying about group communication.

Indirect Service

Indirect service requires hands-on involvement in a service activity without any face-to-face contact with those served. An example would be raising money for a veterans hospital or e-mailing deployed soldiers during your military lessons unit.

Advocacy Service

Advocacy services do not require face-to-face contact with those served. Advocacy involves speaking out on behalf of an issue or cause. For example, starting a school-wide poster campaign to teach others about an issue would be an advocacy service.

Integrating Service Learning

Because the learning should equal the service in service learning, it is important to integrate classroom content with the chosen service. Service learning should reinforce curriculum content and standards for you to benefit academically, personally, and socially. Applying content standard material to real-life experiences will give you a better understanding of the curriculum.

When conducting a service learning project, take time to pinpoint the standards you should address and ways to assess your learning. As a team or class, consider:

- **What standards are we addressing?**
- **What should we know or be able to do?**
- **What assessments can illustrate our learning?**

Key Note Terms

direct service – involves face-to-face contact with those being served in either project or placement models of service learning.

indirect service – requires hands-on involvement in a service activity without any face-to-face contact with those served.

advocacy service – does not require face-to-face contact with those served; involves speaking out on behalf of an issue or cause.

Not only will you fulfill an important need with your service project, you will be learning the national standards in a more relevant and engaging manner.

Service Learning Examples

Field education integrates curriculum programs with service learning. This section presents examples of how you can integrate service learning with curriculum related programs, including:

- **Lions-Quest Skills for Action®**
- **You the People®/Chief Justice®**
- **Groundhog Job Shadow Day®**
- **Cadet Ride®**
- **Winning Colors®**
- **NEFE High School Financial Planning Program®**

Lions-Quest Skills for Action®

Lions-Quest Skills for Action (SFA) is a student-centered program based on combining learning with service. The program is divided into four parts and a Skills Bank. The program curriculum is an elective that advocates service, character, citizenship, and responsibility.

The Skills for Action curriculum helps guide you through the crucial steps of conducting service learning activities. Those steps include identifying needs, choosing and planning a project to address the need, carrying out the project, and reflecting on experiences and exploring what was learned throughout the project.

You the People and Chief Justice®

There are a variety of ways to incorporate service learning with You the People (YTP) and Chief Justice. After you are grounded in YTP citizenship skills and have formed groups, you can identify a service learning activity to integrate into the skill-building curriculum.

For example, you could create, circulate, and publicize a petition that addresses a community issue and create a videotape to document the issue for community officials.

Groundhog Job Shadow Day®

Groundhog Job Shadow Day (GJSD) is a nationwide effort to introduce students to the skills and education needed to make it in today's job market by letting them explore various career options.

For example, you may decide to start a Job Shadow effort to link the schools to the community; then organize a career day or GJSD to make it possible for high school students in the community to explore different career opportunities.

For details about the program, go to *http://www.jobshadow.org.*

Cadet Ride®

The Cadet Ride is an extension of American history that allows you to choose different historical characters to research. You can reenact them on site or in the classroom and then complete a related service learning activity.

You first need to identify issues that still relate to the community today, such as homeless veterans or victims of terrorist attacks; then take time to discuss how you can use what you have learned to improve the community/world issue. Finally, complete a related service learning activity, taking time to reflect on each phase of the experience.

Project examples used with the Cadet Ride include supporting war memorials or assisting in veterans' hospitals or shelters. Specifically, you could decide to educate others on the service of Lieutenant General Maude, who died in the line of duty at the Pentagon on 11 September 2001. In addition, you could plan a memorial for him and/or other victims to commemorate the acts of war that occurred at the World Trade Center, the Pentagon, and in Pennsylvania.

Winning Colors®

Winning Colors states that everyone is capable of developing decision-making, thinking, feeling, and action behaviors. One example of a service learning project would be to teach senior citizens or elementary students about Winning Colors, how to discover their personal needs, and develop a plan to help them achieve a successful balance.

Note

You can earn two hours of college credit with Winning Colors and a service learning project. Ask your JROTC Instructor for more details.

For more information about Winning Colors go to *http://www.winningcolors.com.*

NEFE High School Financial Planning Program®

The National Endowment for Financial Education (NEFE) High School Financial Planning Program® (HSFPP) is designed to teach practical money management skills to introduce financial planning through course work. Numerous service learning activities can be integrated into the NEFE HSFPP curriculum.

> **Note**
>
> You can earn two hours of college credit when you do the NEFE curriculum and a service learning project. Ask your JROTC Instructor for more details.

Suggested service learning activities related to the NEFE HSFPP include:

- **Teach elementary students Junior Achievement material in relation to HSFPP**
- **Provide a budget assistance program**
- **Host a Credit Awareness or Financial Fitness Fair**
- **Develop budgets and spreadsheets for local services**
- **Start an Investment Club in school**
- **Design, produce, and distribute informative posters**
- **Comparison-shop for homebound seniors' groceries**

For more information, call NEFE at (303) 224-3510, or visit *http://www.nefe.org*.

Integration with Additional Unit Content

Besides using applicable curriculum programs in service learning, you may decide to integrate additional content and services. The key is to connect the service activity with course curriculum.

For example, after studying harmful effects of tobacco/drugs, you could teach elementary school kids by putting together an anti-drug advocacy program. You could create banners, skits and instructional materials, then plan and coordinate the elementary program teachings.

After the Service

Key Note Term

after action review – reflecting on what was learned after an act.

After the service, you will participate in an **after action review** so you can reflect, demonstrate, and evaluate. This will be done in three phases, as described in the following sections.

Structured Reflection Phase

Remember, a strong reflection helps develop skills and extend your learning from the service experience. Besides keeping a running learning log of entries, you should hold team discussions to answer open-ended questions before, during, and after each service experience. Sharing what you learned with your teammates and listening to others, will add to your learning experience.

Types of reflection questions to ask about the service learning experience include:

- **Observation**/What—What did I do?
- **Analysis**/So What—What did it mean to me?
- **Integration**/Now What—What will I do because of what I accomplished or learned?

This phase provides you with a structured opportunity to think about what you just did for your community and to describe the feelings that stimulated your actions throughout this activity. Experience indicates that reflection is the key to successful service learning programs.

After you actually perform the service, you should come together as a group to contemplate your service experiences in a project summary report, learning logs, essays, and class discussions. In doing so, you should thoroughly describe what happened during the activity; record any differences your activity actually made; and try to place this experience in a larger context. Specifically, do you believe you successfully accomplished your service learning goals? If not, why? What can you do better the next time? Share your feelings and thoughts. Discuss experiences that made you happy, sad, or angry, events that surprised or frightened you, and other topics related to the activity.

Demonstration Phase

In the demonstration phase, you share with others your mastery of skills, creative ideas, and the outcomes from this project; then identify the next steps to take to benefit the community. The actual demonstration can take many different forms. For example, you might:

- **Give a presentation to peers, faculty, or community members about the activity.**
- **Write articles or letters to local newspapers regarding issues of public concern.**
- **Extend the experience to develop future projects that could benefit the community.**

EVALUATION PHASE: Evaluating Service Learning

A goal in JROTC is to couple high service with high integration of course content to maximize learning and skill development, as well as meet identified needs. When evaluating your service learning activities, reflect upon accomplishments and determine ways to improve.

High service meets a clear and important need and is organized and implemented by students. High integration with curriculum addresses classroom goals, incorporates classroom content, and improves course-related knowledge and skills. Use the following quadrants to rate your service learning experience.

Quadrant 1

Example: After studying financial planning lessons from the National Endowment of Financial Education, cadets teach Junior Achievement lessons to elementary students and assist them in making posters to advocate financial responsibility.

Quadrant 2

Example: Cadets organize a drive for stuffed animals and blankets after learning about work skills and participating in Groundhog Job Shadow Day.

Quadrant 3

Example: Teacher directs cadets to send e-mail to deployed service members after studying a historic event through a cadet ride.

Quadrant 4

Example: Teacher assigns cadets to perform a color guard in the community after studying lessons in You the People.

Service Learning Authentic Assessments

Authentic assessments that evaluate the service activity and student learning are imperative to a successful service learning initiative. Choose assessment tools that measure and affirm learning, program goals, and impact on the need identified, to determine potential improvements.

Service learning lends itself to performance-based assessment, enabling you to exhibit what you have learned in a hands-on and meaningful context. Be sure to take advantage of college credits available through service learning and your curriculum.

Conclusion

In addition to teaching you the value of volunteering, service learning fosters your development of citizenship skills, as well as personal, social and thinking skills. It teaches service responsibilities and prepares future service commitments. Most importantly, service learning builds a spirit of cooperation among you, your peers, the school, and the community.

Chapter 8

Lesson Review

Lesson Review

1. **List the three types of services and give an example of each.**
2. **Choose one service learning curriculum-related program and discuss it.**
3. **Define the term "placement."**
4. **State what you learn through the evaluation phase.**

Index